WHERE ARCHITECTS STAY

LODGINGS FOR DESIGN ENTHUSIASTS

SIBYLLE KRAMER

WHERE ARCHITECTS STAY

LODGINGS
FOR
DESIGN
ENTHUSIASTS

The Deutsche Nationalbibliothek lists this
publication in the Deutsche Nationalbib-
liografie; detailed bibliographic data are
available in the Internet at http://dnb.dnb.de

ISBN 978-3-03768-208-1
© 2017 by Braun Publishing AG
www.braun-publishing.ch

2nd edition 2017

Editor: Sibylle Kramer
Editorial staff and layout:
María Barrera del Amo, Alessia Calabrò
Translation: Cosima Talhouni
Graphic concept: Michaela Prinz, Berlin
Reproduction: Bild1Druck GmbH, Berlin

All of the information in this volume has
been compiled to the best of the editor's
knowledge. It is based on the information
provided to the publisher by the architects'
and designers' offices and excludes any liabil-
ity. The publisher assumes no responsibility
for its accuracy or completeness as well as
copyright discrepancies and refers to the
specified sources (architects' and designers'
offices as well as hosts). All rights to the pho-
tographs are property of the photographer
(please refer to the picture credits).

Contents

Contents

Exterior view of the Manshausen Island Resort.
View of the breakfast room of Casa Talía.

Preface

Architecture and vacation is a combination that promises relaxation and leisure in a perfectly designed surrounding that fulfills almost every wish.

"Where Architects Stay" shows over sixty small and very special such architectural jewels. These charming and unique accommodations are not only a feast for the eyes from an artistic perspective, every project presented here can also be temporarily inhabited. This book is simultaneously an architecture and travel guide. The symbiosis of built architecture and charming surrounding invites visitors to enjoy unforgettable residences apart from mass tourism and away from standard travel destinations and accommodations. Whether isolated,

in a metropolis, near the water, in the mountains or in a city, "Where Architects Stay" shows you enchanting places and carefully designed and detailed objects.

They are much more than just accommodations or houses, they are temporary dream houses that make us forget everyday life and create the perfect foundation for a small get away or a longer break surrounded by poetic and consistently designed architecture.

Get inspired by small archaic designed huts in the mountains, by romantically situated dream houses near lakes, or by luxurious furnished lofts in a city. The large spectrum of selected projects ranges from new constructions via old buildings

Main view of Cabanas no Rio. View out of the Truffle. Night view of the Dune House.

and conversions to sculptural single objects, all distinguished by originality and the masterful utilization of architectural quality. Sometimes the houses make historic references and use present structures like the Cabanas no Rio by Manuel Aires Mateus in Portugal. Small wooden houses formerly used as fishing huts are combined with romantically imbedded objects that are situated directly near the water.

Other times, new buildings are nestled like a pearl necklace at the waterside following its topography. The small houses at Manshausen Island Resort designed by Snorre Stinessen / Stinessen Arkitektur for example, possess a completely glazed front and promise a breathtaking view of the North Sea and Norway's surrounding nature. But architectural pearls for wellness and staying overnight can even be found in big cities, for example the Gorki Apartments, whose interior was designed by Sandra Pauquet, or the newly designed apartment by A-Base in the Oscar-Niemeyer-Haus in Berlin.

Sleep among tree tops in a treehouse or find shelter in a petrified sculpture, an air-raid shelter in Switzerland's mountains, sleep on a houseboat or an old chapel… let yourself be taken on the journey of exploring all of these small architectural jewels.

INFORMATION. ARCHITECTS> OFIS ARCHITECTS AND AKT II, IN COLLABORATION WITH STUDENTS AT HARVARD UNIVERSITY GRADUATE SCHOOL OF DESIGN, FREEAPPROVED AND PD LJUBLJANA MATICA // 2015. SHELTER> 12 SQM // 12 GUESTS. ADDRESS> MOUNTAIN SKUTA, ZGORNJE JEZERSKO, SLOVENIA. WWW.PD-LJMATICA.SI/CABINS/108/ BIVAK-POD-SKUTO-NA-MALIH-PODIH

Alpine Shelter
Skuta

MOUNTAIN SKUTA, SLOVENIA

The project developed from an architectural design studio at the Harvard Graduate School of Design led by Rok Oman and Spela Videcnik from OFIS.

In 2014, thirteen students were asked to design an innovative yet practical shelter to meet the needs of the extreme alpine climate. Inspired by the vernacular architecture of Slovenia with its rich architectural heritage, their proposals, addressing various site conditions, material considerations, and programmatic issues, were produced and cataloged.

The bivouac represents a basic human necessity, a shelter. The outer form and choice of materials respond to the extreme mountain conditions, and also provide views of the magnificent landscape.

Its position in the wilderness demands respect for natural resources, therefore the shelter had to be firmly anchored to the ground with minimal impact. The interior design is modest, subordinate to the function of the shelter providing accommodation for up to eight mountaineers.

Interior view of the timber structure and benches.
Exterior side view. Main view of the shelter from
below. Night view.

View from above. Detail of the larch timber interior.
View of the large lit structural window. Cross section.
Main view of the shelter composed by the three
pre-built modules.

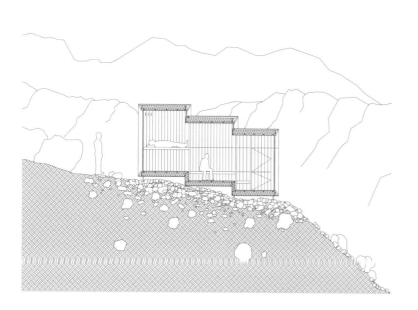

GETTING AROUND. A DESTINA-
TION FOR HIKERS AND CLIMBERS IN
ALL SEASONS, THE SITE WITH THE
EXISTING SHELTER IS LOCATED UNDER
THE SKUTA MOUNTAIN IN KAMNIŠKE
ALPE, SLOVENIA AT AN ELEVATION
OF 2,070 METERS. IT SITS ALONG AN
UNMARKED TRAIL LEADING TO THE
SUMMIT OF SKUTA WITH AN ALTITUDE
OF 2,532 METERS. EACH YEAR A FEW
HUNDRED MOUNTAINEERS AND HIK-
ERS STOP AT THE SHELTER, SOME FOR
THE NIGHT, SOME ONLY FOR A BRIEF
BREAK. THE SITE IS VALUED FOR ITS
SPECTACULAR VIEWS.

INFORMATION. ARCHITECT>
SANDRA PAUQUET // 2013.
APARTMENT BUILDING>
34 APARTMENTS + 2 PENTHOUSES.
ADDRESS> WEINBERGSWEG 25,
BERLIN, GERMANY.
WWW.GORKIAPARTMENTS.COM

Dining area of the Gorki Apartments' Penthouse 2.
Main entrance of the apartment building
Dining room Penthouse 1, featuring a large window
and wooden floor.

View of the master bedroom in Penthouse 2,
through the big glass door. Bathroom with
black and white wallpaper and tile floor.
View of the Categorki 2C kitchen.

Gorki
Apartments

BERLIN, GERMANY

The Gorki Apartments embody the unique flair of their neighborhood both inside and out. Housed in the inconspicuous frame of a turn-of-the-19th-century building on a tree-lined street, the 36-apartment accommodation presents an unconventional and distinctly Berlin concept of luxury. Guests won't find a lobby when they enter the massive doors of the Gorki. Instead, they walk through a lush courtyard to the refined and homey reception office, evoking the comfort of a private residence.

Together with the architecture firm Fuchshuber & Partner, French-German architect Sandra Pauquet in collaboration with Kim Wang and his team set out to give the historic building new life. The Gorki today

is a pastiche of patina walls, high ceilings, original crown moldings and open floor plans typical of Berlin apartments. The 34 guest apartments and two penthouses represent Sandra Pauquet's unique vision of unconventional luxury. Paying homage to the former residents of the buildings, traditional room numbers are forgone. Instead, each room is assigned a fictional name such as Lea Grün or Herr Günther, which is also etched into the apartment key. With its own doorbell and mailbox, each apartment feels like a pied-à-terre or the home of a stylish friend – with all the comforts of a luxury hotel, from a full-service concierge to daily room cleaning.

Master bedroom of Penthouse 2. Bedroom and dining area of the Categorki 2B apartments.

Rooftop terrace of Penthouse 1. Warm tones and wooden details for another sleeping area. Detail of the green bathroom with gray wallpaper. Penthouse 1 floor plan.

GETTING AROUND. GORKI APARTMENTS OFFERS ITS GUESTS BIKES TO EXPLORE THE CITY. LOCATED ON WEINBERGSWEG NEAR ROSENTHALER PLATZ, RESIDENTS CAN MINGLE WITH THE YOUNG START-UP SOCIETY THAT BROUGHT SILICON VALLEY FLAIR TO BERLIN. ROSENTHALER PLATZ IS A GREAT STARTING POINT TO EXPLORE THE ENTIRE CITY. EVERY DESTINATION CAN BE REACHED EASILY BY PUBLIC TRANSPORTATION. SHOPPING, DINING, AND MANY OF THE CITY'S HISTORICAL SITES ARE JUST A STONE'S THROW AWAY.

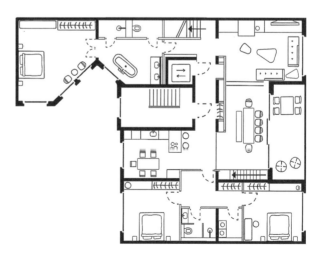

General view of the house. View of the floor with
wooden walls and ceiling

INFORMATION. ARCHITECTS>
ACME // 2010. HOUSE> 213 SQM //
10 GUESTS // 5 BEDROOMS //
3 BATHROOMS. ADDRESS> HUNSETT
MILL, CHAPEL FIELD ROAD, STALHAM,
NORFOLK, ENGLAND.
WWW.HUNSETTMILL.CO.UK

Mill House

STALHAM, ENGLAND

Hunsett Mill is a water pumping
mill located in the historic Norfolk
Broads National Park, England.
The house was the residence of
the mill keeper until 1900, when
electricity rendered wind-powered
pumps obsolete. Since then, the
house was used as a private
residence, but has remained an
important piece of local heritage.

The house was expanded 5 times
in the 20th century, with each
extension adding on new rooms like
kitchen, bathroom and bedroom,
but the resulting agglomeration
of extensions was esthetically and
functionally of very low quality.
The client requested an enlarge-
ment of the house to create more
open living spaces and two additional bedrooms. Rather than

adding more extensions, all previous
extensions were demolished and
the cottage returned to its original
shape, with only one new extension
added in the back.

In order for the new extension to
retreat behind the listed setting of
the mill, the new addition was conceived as a shadow of the existing
house. By adding a dark volume to
the existing brick volume and by
virtue of the chosen façade geome-
try, the exact shape of the extension
volume seems ambiguous from afar.

GETTING AROUND. HUNSETT MILL HAS A WONDERFULLY QUIET AND PEACEFUL LOCATION WITH A LARGE PRIVATE GARDEN ON THE BANKS OF THE RIVER ANT. THERE IS PLENTY OF NATURAL WILDLIFE TO ENJOY IN THE GARDEN AND THE PROTECTED MARSHLAND ALL AROUND. GREAT WALKS RANGE FROM LONG, EMPTY BEACHES TO BLOWY CLIFFTOPS, BOARDWALKS THROUGH CONSERVED REED LANDS AND WETLANDS. THE PICTURESQUE TOWNS OF NORTH NORFOLK AND THE CITY OF NORWICH ARE NEARBY.

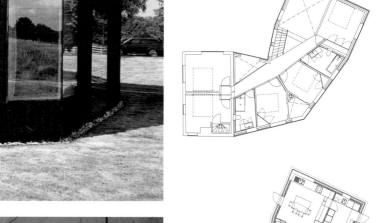

Exterior view of the black extension with irregular windows. One of the bedrooms. Floor plans.

INFORMATION. ARCHITECTS> ENSAMBLE STUDIO // 2010. CABIN> 25 SQM // 2 GUESTS // 1 BEDROOM // 1 BATHROOM. ADDRESS> COSTA DA MORTE, GALICIA, SPAIN. WWW.ENSAMBLE.INFO

View of the surrounding nature from the bed.
Stone fireplace.

The Truffle

COSTA DA MORTE, SPAIN

The Truffle is a piece of nature built of earth and filled with air. A space within a stone that sits on the ground and blends with the territory. To build it, a hole was dug in the ground, and the removed topsoil piled up on its perimeter, obtaining a retaining dike. Then a volume of hay bales was built and placed in the hole and the space between it and the earth flooded with poured concrete to solidify it. After some time, the earth was removed to uncover an amorphous mass. The earth had provided the concrete with texture, color, form, and essence, and in return the concrete gave the earth its strength and internal structure.

However, the result was a stone, not yet architecture. It was cut open to explore its core and it was found that the hay mass inside it had become compressed by the hydrostatic pressure exerted by the concrete. To empty the interior, the calf Paulina enjoyed the nicest hay for a year until she left weighing 300 kilograms. She had eaten the interior volume of hay, and empty space appeared for the first time, constituting the architecture of the Truffle that had sheltered the animal and the vegetable mass for a long time.

GETTING AROUND. THE TRUFFLE SITS IN A RURAL GALICIAN LANDSCAPE, NEAR THE O CAMIÑO DOS FAROS (THE WAY OF LIGHTHOUSES), A 200-KILOMETER HIKING ROUTE ALONG THE COAST. THE REGION ALSO FEATURES THE FISHING VILLAGES OF COSTA DA MORTE, MEGALITHIC MONUMENTS AND LOCAL GASTRONOMY, WHILE THE HISTORIC CITY OF SANTIAGO DE COMPOSTELA IS AROUND 50 KILOMETERS AWAY.

Main view of the Truffle. Interior view. Floor plan. Detail of the shower and small washbasin.

INFORMATION. ARCHITECTS>
DIECKMANN SATZIGER ARCHITEKTEN
AND MARK POHL // 2012.
APARTMENTS> 110 SQM, 105 SQM
AND 45 SQM // FROM 2 TO 8 GUESTS //
FROM 1 TO 3 BEDROOMS EACH //
1 BATHROOM EACH. ADDRESS>
FULDAER STR. 85, WEIMAR, GERMANY.
WWW.HIERWARGOETHENIE.DE

Design Apartments Weimar

WEIMAR, GERMANY

The unique holiday rental concept of the Design Apartments Weimar allows visitors to enjoy a vacation, design, and shopping. The Design Apartments Weimar were established in 2012 and consist of three apartments managed by Mark Pohl and Udo Joerke.

Built in 1907, the historical complex was returned to its original state during the detailed high-quality renovation with timber windows, hardwood floors, and loam rendering walls in the years 2009–2011. A 50-square-meter apartment is located on the attic floor with a roof terrace, while two 105-square-meter apartments below are complete with loggias and balconies. The interior design is a mix of classic design pieces, flea market treasures, and modern design elements.

Guests staying at the Design Apartments Weimar actually experience a "live-in showroom" in which they can experience affordable design in the form of small series and unique objects that they can purchase on location or online at www.designwe. love.

View of the entrance and sleeping area. Dining room. View of the little loggia on the last floor. Living and dining area.

Bedroom. View of the large corridor with wooden floor. Floor plan of one of the three apartments.

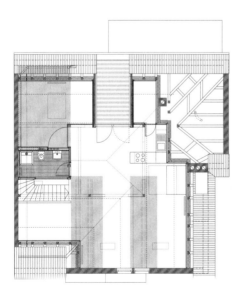

GETTING AROUND. THE BIRTHPLACE OF BAUHAUS AND HOME OF ITS FOUNDER, ARCHITECT WALTER GROPIUS, WEIMAR WAS THE EUROPEAN CITY OF CULTURE IN 1999. IT HAS BEEN THE RESIDENCE OF FAMOUS GERMAN WRITERS GOETHE AND SCHILLER, AS WELL AS KAFKA AND NIETZSCHE; COMPOSERS JOHANN SEBASTIAN BACH AND FRANZ LISZT; ARTIST LUCAS CRANACH AND ARTIST, ARCHITECT AND DESIGNER HENRY VAN DE VELDE. WEIMAR ALSO OFFERS BEAUTIFUL SITES ON ITS OUTSKIRTS, SUCH AS THE CASTLES BELVEDERE AND ETTERSBERG.

Workplace and living room. Relax area.
Detail of the little loggia.

INFORMATION. ARCHITECT> CUMULUS STUDIO // 2014. BOUTIQUE HOTEL> 1,035 SQM // 36 GUESTS // 18 SUITES // 18 BATHROOMS. ADDRESS> LAKE ST. CLAIR ROAD, LAKE ST. CLAIR, TASMANIA, AUSTRALIA. WWW.PUMPHOUSEPOINT.COM.AU

Pumphouse Point

LAKE ST. CLAIR, TASMANIA, AUSTRALIA

Located just inside the Tasmanian Wilderness World Heritage Area, Pumphouse Point was originally constructed as part of Tasmania's hydroelectric scheme and had been abandoned for over twenty years before being redeveloped through the adaptive reuse and refurbishment of two existing, heritage listed, off-form concrete art deco buildings – "The Pumphouse" and "The Shorehouse" – into a wilderness retreat.

Eighteen new guest suites, communal lounge areas, and a shared dining area were inserted into the existing off-form concrete building envelopes. From inception, the architects envisaged that Pumphouse Point should encapsulate rugged simplicity and unrefined comfort.

Through its design, it builds on the sense of arrival and place inherent in the unique location, whilst alluding to the site's history through material selection and construction detailing. In keeping with best heritage practice and the values of the World Heritage Area in which it is located, the design is focused on environmental stewardship, sustainability and minimal site impact.

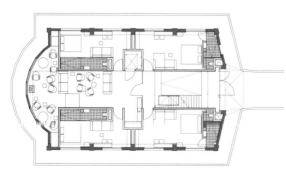

GETTING AROUND. PUMPHOUSE POINT IS LOCATED AT THE SOUTHERN END OF LAKE ST. CLAIR, WITHIN THE TASMANIAN WILDERNESS WORLD HERITAGE AREA AT THE EDGE OF THE CRADLE MOUNTAIN – LAKE ST. CLAIR NATIONAL PARK. THE CONVERTED PUMPHOUSE APPEARS TO FLOAT ON TOP OF THE LAKE – AUSTRALIA'S DEEPEST – AND SITS AT THE END OF A 250-METER CONCRETE FLUME, WHICH IS ITS ONLY CONNECTION TO LAND. THE LOCATION ENCOURAGES GUESTS TO EXPLORE THE SURROUNDINGS BY FOOT, BOAT OR BIKE, AND DISCOVER THE LOCAL WILDLIFE.

Common area with view of the lake. First and ground floor plans. View of the staircase with rough-sawn timber walls.

Interior view of a typical suite. Common dining area. Night view.

INFORMATION. ARCHITECT>
ARQUITECTURA ANNA NOGUERA //
2009. HOUSE> 594 SQM // 10 GUESTS
// 5 BEDROOMS // 5 BATHROOMS.
ADDRESS> CARRER DELS ALEMANYS 5,
GIRONA, SPAIN.
WWW.ALEMANYS5.COM

View of the kitchen and dining area from the covered balcony. The garden with a palette of steel, concrete and stone details. Fireplace and large window in the living space.

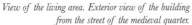
View of the living area. Exterior view of the building from the street of the medieval quarter.

Alemanys 5

GIRONA, SPAIN

The restoration of the 16th-century building was a search for the most intrinsic characteristics of the original construction, and freeing it from additions and recent renovations, interpreting the old elements not so much through a historical perspective as through their architectural qualities.

The minimalism of the intervention suggests the austerity of past times. The new work dialogues with the old. The entry of natural light helps to shape the volumes and emphasizes the fluidity of the spaces. The renovation involved very few materials: stone, wood, steel and concrete, with their natural colors and textures.

The architectural unit consists of the body of the building and a side garden facing the street. The building has two arms, the first one aligned with the street and the other with the thick interior wall. The staircase, positioned in the space in between these two bodies, acts as a pivotal point from which the rest of the layout is generated.

*View of the dining area. Sleeping area with the
original stone walls. Detail of the staircase.
View of the garden and the pool. Floor plans.*

GETTING AROUND. GIRONA IS A
SMALL CHARMING CITY LOCATED
100 KILOMETERS NORTH OF BARCE-
LONA. IT HAS ONE OF THE MOST
IMPORTANT MEDIEVAL QUARTERS IN
SPAIN, IN WHICH THE HOUSE IS LO-
CATED. THE CITY OFFERS A VIBRANT
SHOPPING DISTRICT AND DIVERSE
CULTURAL LIFE WHICH CAN ALL BE EN-
JOYED BY FOOT. THE AREA AROUND
THE CITY IS SUITABLE FOR BICYCLING,
GOLFING, AND SKIING. IT IS ALSO
RENOWNED AS A WELLNESS AND SPA
AREA AND AN EXQUISITE CULINARY
DESTINATION.

INFORMATION. ARCHITECT>
MANUEL AIRES MATEUS // 2013.
HUT> 26 SQM // 2 GUESTS //
1 BEDROOM // 1 BATHROOM.
ADDRESS> SÍTIO DA CARRASQUEIRA,
COMPORTA, PORTUGAL.
WWW.CABANASNORIO.COM

Main view of the huts. View from the jetty.

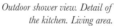
*Outdoor shower view. Detail of
the kitchen. Living area.*

Cabanas
no Rio

COMPORTA, PORTUGAL

This project, by architect Manuel Aires Mateus, is based on the concept of "use/reuse and recycle" using two old fishermen huts to create a romantic refuge, surrounded by nature, offering visitors a genuine experience of Comporta, Portugal.

The two small huts, of fourteen square meters each, were both built off-site and transported to Comporta. "The wharf is medieval and assembled from wood", said the architect. "Its identity allows it to change and to replace, while keeping all its values". The construction is entirely finished in "costaneiros" wood, the first and last boards sawn from a log. The structures are then submitted to the climate, giving them a unique personality.

Cabanas no Rio was created for two visitors. The first cabin contains the bedroom with en-suite bathroom and shower, which can be used outdoors and indoors. The second cabin contains the living room with a small kitchen equipped to prepare simple meals.

Exterior view of the hut with the bedroom.
General view with the natural reserve of river Sado
at the background. Detail of the bed. Frontal view.
Floor plans.

GETTING AROUND. CABANAS NO RIO IS 1 HOUR SOUTH FROM LISBON IN THE VILLAGE OF COMPORTA, PORTUGAL. THE NATURAL RESERVE OF RIVER SADO IS A TRUE NATURAL PARADISE THAT OFFERS VISITORS BEAUTIFUL WHITE SANDY BEACHES, GREEN RICE FIELDS, AND TYPICAL FISHERMEN'S HOUSES. THE TWO CABINS WITH PITCHED ROOFS ARE ON THE RIVERBANK, NEXT A SMALL JETTY ON STILTS. THE SITE OFFERS A VIEW OF THE PALAFITTE HARBOR OF CAR-RASQUEIRA, A UNIQUE MASTERPIECE OF FOLK ARCHITECTURE.

INFORMATION. FURNITURE PRODUCER, DESIGNER> NILS HOLGER MOORMANN // 2008. APARTMENT BUILDING> 14 APARTMENTS + 2 CABINS. ADDRESS> KAMPENWANDSTRASSE 85, ASCHAU IM CHIEMGAU, GERMANY. WWW.MOORMANN-BERGE.DE

Detail of the kitchen and dining corner of one of the apartments. Sleeping area.

Guesthouse Berge

ASCHAU IM CHIEMGAU, GERMANY

The charming Guesthouse Berge is nestled in Aschau im Chiemgau, at the foot of the Kampenwand mountain. It does not offer excessive luxury – but rather an inviting ambiance, natural materials, real art, and great attention to details.

Almost all apartments are equipped with a small, but smart kitchen, but excellent food is also offered by the Berge chefs. The served food is for the most part organically or regionally grown. When redesigning the listed building that has received several international design awards, owner Nils Holger Moormann focused on the individual character of each room.

The historical substance was retained where possible, and placed in stark contrast to a modern, reduced design. The charming result includes creaking hardwood floors that encounter untreated steel, and clay walls and open stonework that meet large glass façades. Instead of a television, each quarter offers a large selection of books.

GETTING AROUND. THE CLIMATIC SPA ASCHAU IM CHIEMGAU WITH ITS SNOWY RETREAT "MOUNTAIN VILLAGE" OF SACHRANG (738 METERS) IS LOCATED BETWEEN MUNICH AND SALZBURG, KAISER MOUNTAINS, AND THE BAVARIAN SEA. THE TRIDENT ROCKY BACKDROP OF THE 1,669-METER HIGH KAMPENWAND AND THE HOHENASCHAU CASTLE RESIDING OVER THE PRIEN VALLEY ARE THE LANDMARKS OF THIS VENERABLE PICTURESQUE CULTURE-SEEPED AREA THAT HAS BEEN A POPULAR SUMMER VACATION SPOT FOR MORE THAN 100 YEARS.

View of the wooden kitchen island. The custom-designed family bed niche. Dining area. View from the garden.

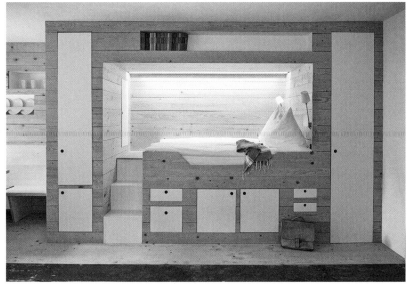

39

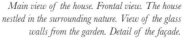

Main view of the house. Frontal view. The house nestled in the surrounding nature. View of the glass walls from the garden. Detail of the façade.

Mirror Houses

BOLZANO, ITALY

The Mirror Houses are a pair of holiday homes set in the marvelous surroundings of the South Tyrolean Dolomites, amidst beautiful scenery of apple orchards, just outside the city of Bolzano. The client, who lives in a restructured farmhouse of the 1960s on the site, asked to design a structure for renting out as luxury holiday units providing maximum privacy for both the client and the residing guests. Each unit contains a kitchen / living room as well as a bath- and bedroom with big skylights that provide natural light and ventilation.

The project's initial volume is split into two units that are slightly shifted in height and length to articulate each unit. Both units float on a base above the ground evoking lightness while offering magnificent views from their cantilevered terraces.

The old existing farmhouse is mirrored in the new contemporary architecture and literally blends into it rather than compete against it.

INFORMATION. ARCHITECT>
PETER PICHLER ARCHITECTURE // 2014.
RESIDENTIAL UNITS> 40 SQM PER UNIT
// 2 GUESTS PER UNIT // 1 BEDROOM
EACH // 1 BATHROOM EACH.
ADDRESS> VIA AGRUZZO 75,
BOLZANO, ITALY.
WWW.MIRROR-HOUSES.COM

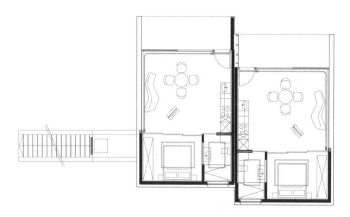

GETTING AROUND. THE MIRROR HOUSES ARE LOCATED IN SOUTH TYROL IN NORTHERN ITALY. THE REGION'S 505,000 INHABITANTS SPEAK THREE DIFFERENT LANGUAGES: GERMAN, ITALIAN AND LADIN, AN ANCIENT RHAETO-ROMANCE LANGUAGE. SOUTH TYROL IS FAMOUS FOR ITS BREATHTAKING LANDSCAPES, CULINARY DELIGHTS, ESPECIALLY ITS EXQUISITE WINES AND COUNTLESS POSSIBILITIES FOR OUTDOOR ACTIVITIES. IN NUMBERS, THERE ARE 51,000 SQUARE KILOMETERS OF VINEYARDS OFFERING WHITE AND RED WINE, 30 SKI RESORTS, 380 KILOMETERS OF BIKE TRACKS, AND 350 MOUNTAIN PEAKS.

*Main view from the garden. Ground floor plan.
Detail of the mirror façade. View of the white
living room.*

*Detail of window and black façade. View from
the garden of the small entrance terrace.*

GETTING AROUND. LIBERTINE LINDENBERG IS EMBEDDED IN THE HISTORIC APPLE CIDER DISTRICT OF FRANKFURT: IN ALT-SACHSENHAUSEN TRADITION MEETS AVANT-GARDE, MEAT AND SAUSAGE PLATTERS MEET STREET FOOD, AND LOCAL PUBS MEET STYLISH BARS. IN ADDITION TO THE OLD ESTABLISHED PUBS AND BARS, THE INFAMOUS CHARM OF THE COBBLESTONE DISTRICT INCREASINGLY ATTRACTS ARTISTS, DESIGNERS, AND CREATIVE INDIVIDUALS. IN THE PAST FEW YEARS THE NEARBY STREETS HAVE BECOME STOMPING GROUNDS FOR LOVERS OF CONTEMPORARY SHOPPING AND DINING CONCEPTS.

View of the duplex with kitchenette. Exterior view of the building. View of the suite with black hole corner.

View of the common area. View of the suite.
Details of the entrance and living-room-café.

INFORMATION. ARCHITECTS>
FRANKEN ARCHITEKTEN AND
STUDIO KATHI KAEPPEL // 2016.
HOTEL> 1,550 SQM // 55–70 GUESTS //
27 SUITES // 27 BATHROOMS.
ADDRESS> FRANKENSTEINER STRASSE
20, FRANKFURT AM MAIN, GERMANY.
WWW.DAS-LINDENBERG.DE

LIBERTINE LINDENBERG

FRANKFURT AM MAIN, GERMANY

LIBERTINE LINDENBERG is neither a hotel nor a living community. Yet it is both: a guest community. At its home in the district of Alt-Sachsenhausen in Frankfurt, LIBERTINE invites guests to stay in a timeless setting. Overnight guests are as welcome as those who are looking for a second home for days, months, or even years.

LIBERTINE firmly believes that her guests should not hesitate to fall in love: with the one to three room suites of its Wilhelminian style house, guests can enjoy a lovely refuge in the heart of the district with a view of Frankfurt's skyline. In her common rooms, LIBERTINE has made plenty of room for new friendships. Here her guests can roam freely whenever and as often as they feel like it.

Whoever lives at LIBERTINE may determine the desired level of service, whether it means having the newspaper delivered, receiving a shoeshine, or enjoying a relaxing massage. Of course, guests can cook for themselves, do their own laundry or go grocery shopping. LIBERTINE's guests are always free to decide.

Aufberg 1110

PIESENDORF, AUSTRIA

Aufberg 1110 with its two exclusive apartments is located in the midst of the High Tauern region with a magnificent view of the mountains. The house pays tribute to its neighbor, yet remains independent. Together they create a special venue on the mountain.

The simple structure seems to be naturally carved out of the rock with its roof reflecting the same steep slope. The house is entirely made out of wood, rendering it ecological and sustainable. The raw larch wood cladding allows the house to age with dignity while also giving it a warm atmosphere on the inside and outside.

The interior is unexpectedly spacious. Two apartments with galleries are located at different heights. At the same time, the windows frame the view of the landscape and create a flowing transition between indoors and outdoors. The open fireplace and the warm larch wood create a protective chalet atmosphere that is very comforting.

Main view at night. Bedroom with large window and wooden furniture. Side view of the house.

INFORMATION. ARCHITECTS>
MECK ARCHITEKTEN, ANDREAS MECK
AND AXEL FRÜHAUF // 2012. HOUSE>
2 APARTMENTS // 6 GUESTS //
2 BEDROOMS // 2 BATHROOMS.
ADDRESS> DÜRNBERG 267,
5721 PIESENDORF, AUSTRIA.
WWW.AUFBERG.AT

Bedroom with bathtub. Detail of the stairway.
View out of the dining and living room area. Section.
General view of the house.

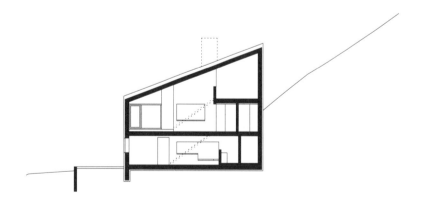

GETTING AROUND. THE EUROPEAN
SPORTS REGION ZELL AM SEE-KAPRUN
OFFERS UNLIMITED SPORTS ACTIVI-
TIES YEAR-ROUND. AT THE SAME TIME,
THE AUFBERG IS THE IDEAL START-
ING POINT FOR VARIOUS DAY TRIPS.
NEARBY ATTRACTIONS INCLUDE
THE BAROQUE CITY OF SALZBURG,
THE ROMANTIC KITZLOCHKLAMM,
THE KRIMML WATERFALLS, AND THE
UNIQUE PANORAMIC ROAD TO THE
GROSSGLOCKNER, AUSTRIA'S HIGH-
EST MOUNTAIN.

INFORMATION. ARCHITECTS AND DESIGNERS> ARCHIWORKSHOP, HEE-JUN SIM AND SU-JEONG PARK // 2013. TENT> 37 SQM AND 53 SQM // 2 GUESTS PER GLAMPING // 1 BEDROOM // 1 BATHROOM. ADDRESS> YANGPYEONG-GUN, GYEONGGI-DO, SEOUL, SOUTH KOREA. WWW.ARCHIWORKSHOP.KR

Main view of the "Modular Flow" units. View from the bordering forest. General view of the two types of Glamping units.

Glamping Architectures

SEOUL, SOUTH KOREA

Why not create a glamping site that gives people a chance to experience nature up close while also enjoying a uniquely designed architecture experience? These questions led to the creation of Glamping Architecture in Korea – a location in which nature, ecological values, comfort, and modern design are all combined into an exciting adventure.

There are two types of Glamping units. Stacking Doughnut unit is inspired by pebble stones, while Modular Flow unit is designed for extendable structures by juxtaposing modular floor panels.

The idea behind stacking Doughnut and Modular Flow units is to offer high-standard accommodation in a variety of places.

These are called sea, desert, creek, mountain, cave, forest, river and city.

GETTING AROUND. GLAMPING ARCHITECTURE BY ARCHIWORKSHOP OFFERS A UNIQUE CAMPING EXPERIENCE. TWO TYPES OF GLAMPING UNITS WITH CONTEMPORARY DESIGN ARE POSITIONED IN THE MIDDLE OF THE GENTLE KOREAN NATURE. FROM THE GLAMPING SITE, YOU HAVE A VIEW OF A LUSH VALLEY, MILES OF FOREST AND A NEARBY STREAM.

Sleeping area with wall painted by a young korean artist. View of the "Doughnut" units. Exterior view of the covering membrane.

Detail of the patio in the "Doughnut" tent type. Frontal view. Night view of the tents.

INFORMATION. ARCHITECTS> STUDIOMAMA // 2012. TOWNHOUSE> 38 SQM // 4 GUESTS // 1 BEDROOM // 1 BATHROOM. ADDRESS> VOSS STREET, LONDON, ENGLAND. WWW.AIRBNB.CO.UK/ROOMS/2388750

Voss Street 2

LONDON, ENGLAND

Voss Street 2 is a townhouse for short or longer stays in London. Once a carpenter's workshop, it has been transformed into a multi-level tailor-made living space, entirely consisting of unique design elements built by local crafts people. Designed by Jack Mama and Nina Tolstrup, the furniture was custom-designed or hacked for this location, using mainly recycled materials giving the space an urban stylish Scandinavian feel.

The space is playful and offers a full spec hand built kitchen with quality appliances and utensils. The living area is on the ground floor and one floor up is comprised of a bed pod, lounge with work area and customized molded bathroom. Suspended above this area is a hanging pod

in the form of a mini house. The entire scheme both internally and externally was carefully designed to preserve the integrity of the existing structure.

Situated in the heart of the historic East End, Voss Street is a cobble-stone alley off the Bethnal Green Road that connects Spitalfields and the famous curry destination Brick Lane to the east and the delightful Bethnal Green. With its cobblestone and market trader lock ups it has had many different incarnations.

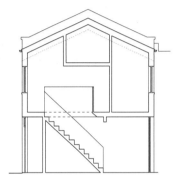

GETTING AROUND. THE AREA HAS BECOME A KEY ALTERNATIVE CREATIVE CENTER IN LONDON. YOU CAN FIND GRAND NEWCOMERS AND REVERED INSTITUTIONS, HUMBLE HOLES-IN-THE-WALL AND GAUDY OLD PUBS, ALL OF WHICH OFFER SOMETHING THAT SETS THEM APART FROM THE MUNDANE AND FLY-BY-NIGHT. A CULTURAL MELTING POT, BETHNAL GREEN IS HOME TO A DIVERSE MIX OF PEOPLE MAKING IT A FOOD LOVER'S PARADISE. VISITORS THAT ARE MORE SPIRITED WILL FIND AN ARRAY OF MUSIC VENUES AND INNOVATIVE CLUBS.

View of the custom-designed bed. View of the bedroom. Section. View of the living area.

GETTING AROUND. THE BAITA IS JUST 100 METERS FROM A CABLE CAR GOING UP INTO THE HEART OF THE VIA LATTEA'S 400 KILOMETERS OF DOWNHILL SLOPES, INCLUDING SEVERAL OLYMPIC RUNS. FOR THOSE SEEKING MORE OF A WORK-OUT, THE 2006 OLYMPIC CROSS-COUNTRY SKIING COURSE IS THE SAME DISTANCE FROM THE FRONT DOOR. THERE IS A GOLF COURSE WITHIN A 10 MINUTES' WALK AND SESTRIERE OFFERS MANY FOOD AND NIGHTLIFE OPTIONS. THE HISTORY OF THE REGION CAN BE EXPLORED AT VARIOUS NATIONAL MONUMENTS AND WALKS, INCLUDING THE IMPRESSIVE FENESTRELLE FORT.

View of the living room. One of the bedrooms.
View of the dining area with vaulted stone ceilings.

Relaxing area opening onto a roof terrace with a hot tub and a view of the Mountain. View of the kitchen. Floor plan.

INFORMATION. ARCHITECT> DANIELE RONCHAIL. DESIGNER> LUCIE MCCULLOUGH // 2010. CHALET> 450 SQM // 12 ADULTS + 6 KIDS // 6 BEDROOMS // 5 ½ BATHROOMS. ADDRESS> FRAZIONE PATTEMOUCHE, PRAGELATO, PIEDMONT, ITALY. WWW.BAITA1697.COM

Baita 1697

PRAGELATO, ITALY

Lucie McCullough, the owner and interior designer of Baita 1697, stumbled upon an old hidden stone farmhouse, or "baita" in the local dialect, near the ski resort of Sestriere. The 17th-century house was built in the traditional way.

Observing the strict Italian building laws, designed to protect and preserve the architectural legacy of the area, the house ended up combining the best of the original features of the structure: beautiful vaulted stone ceilings in the ground floor, the original ceiling in what is now the kitchen, and most of the original wood; with some additions: a terrace cut into the traditional stone-flagged roof, with floor-to-ceiling windows, a hot tub on the terrace, and a large copper bathtub in one of the bedrooms. Baita 1697 provided a home for the family, and a place to welcome friends – the six bedrooms and kids' dorm provide plenty of accommodation, while multiple living areas provide ample opportunity to be a part of the crowd or to find a quiet corner.

GETTING AROUND. LA MELAGRANA IS AN IDEAL PLACE FOR A VACATION IN NATURE, NEAR THE SEA, WITH THE CHANCE TO VISIT BAROQUE ART SITES OF EXTRAORDINARY ELEGANCE. IT IS LOCATED ONLY 5 KILOMETERS FROM THE CITY OF NOTO AND 15 MINUTES FROM THE GOLDEN BEACHES AT THE NATURAL RESERVE OF VENDICARI. VAL DI NOTO IS ONE OF THE MOST SPECTACULAR BAROQUE ART SITES IN SICILY, WHICH WAS LISTED AS A WORLD HERITAGE SITE BY UNESCO IN 2002.

Main view of the house from below. The sleeping area with a large window. The terrace with a panoramic view. Details of the living area.

INFORMATION. ARCHITECT> MARIA GIUSEPPINA GRASSO CANNIZZO // 2010. HOUSE> 115 SQM // 6 GUESTS // 3 BEDROOMS // 2 BATHROOMS. ADDRESS> NOTO, SICILY, ITALY. WWW.LA-MELAGRANA.IT/EN/

La Melagrana

SICILY, ITALY

La melagrana, nestled in the countryside just a few kilometers from Noto, blends in perfectly with the surrounding landscape thanks to its basic and subtle forms.

The home, characterized by large windows, offers guests a vast view of the countryside and the natural reserve of Vendicari, across fields of olive and almond trees and citrus orchards, all the way to the sea. The interiors are detailed, characterized by vintage design furnishings alongside contemporary and custom-made pieces.

The home consists of a stationary body (the owner's home) and a mobile one (intended for guests), which runs along tracks anchored to the load-bearing structure of the terrace. When closed, it acts as an anti-intrusion barrier; while opened it leaves room for a spacious terrace overlooking the countryside and the sea. The large covered terrace, which is the main feature of the building, protrudes into the park and the former barnyard, now equipped with lounge chairs and table, allows pleasant relaxation in the shade.

INFORMATION. ARCHITECT> FEUERSINGER ARCHITEKTUR // 2015. HOUSE> 230 SQM // 10 + 2 GUESTS // 5 BEDROOMS // 4 BATHROOMS + 1 SHOWER IN THE SAUNA. ADDRESS> SENNINGERFELD 8, BRAMBERG AM WILDKOGEL, AUSTRIA. WWW.AUFDALEITN8.AT

Exterior winter view with snow.
View of the chill area and the terrace.
Living and dining area with fireplace
and large windows.

Auf da Leitn 8

BRAMBERG AM WILDKOGEL, AUSTRIA

Auf da Leitn 8 is located in the heart of the High Tauern region right next to a skiing track in the midst of a vehicle-free hamlet 819 meters above sea level. The spirit of local chalets is reflected in a novel and understated way in the natural stone façade, larch wood shingles, and oak wood interior.

The straight-lined design does not make the ambiance seem rustic but modern instead. Precise lines dominate the furniture and the only ornaments are found on the chairs that were made by hand based on traditional templates that grant the interior the right amount of a local touch.

The wood shimmers in different hues depending on the light and livens up the rooms. The Corten steel cladding on the terraces is exposed to the seasons and develops a color range of its own. Up to twelve people can be comfortably accommodated in the 230-square-meter living space across three floors.

Main view of the house from the garden.
Detail of the internal wood coverings.

Living and dining area with wooden furniture.
View of the bathroom. Detail of the façade.
Ground floor plan.

GETTING AROUND. WINTER ATTRAC-
TIONS INCLUDE SKIING AND SLED-
DING RIGHT OUTSIDE THE DOOR , SKI
TOURS, ICE SKATING, SNOW HIKING,
CROSS COUNTRY SKIING. NEARBY
SKIING AREAS INCLUDE KITZBÜHEL
PASS THURN (WORLD'S BEST SKI
RESORT), ZILLERTALARENA, AND
KITZSTEINHORN. SUMMER ATTRAC-
TIONS INCLUDE HIKING, CLIMBING,
MOUNTAIN BIKING, PARAGLIDING,
SWIMMING, GOLFING, THE KRIMMLER
WATERFALLS, AND THE CITIES OF
SALZBURG, INNSBRUCK, AND MUNICH,
WHICH CAN BE REACHED IN ABOUT
1.5 HOURS.

INFORMATION. ARCHITECTS>
CADAVAL & SOLÀ-MORALES // 2012.
HOUSE> 250 SQM // 1 BEDROOM //
1 BATHROOM. ADDRESS>
TEPOZTLÁN, MORELOS, MEXICO.
WWW.AIRBNB.COM

*Main view of the house from the swimming pool.
View of the sleeping area with fireplace. View from
the garden.*

Tepoztlán Lounge

TEPOZTLÁN, MEXICO

Located in an amazing landscape, the Tepoztlán Lounge is the first completed building of a larger project that also includes a series of bungalows of different sizes and designs, which can be rented by the year, month, or day.

Located in the perimeter of a magnificent lawn, the lounge is a central public space for leisure in nature. The idiosyncrasy of the project relies on the contrast of the carefully manicured lawn with the wild nature in the boundaries of this central space. The project is a negotiation between interior and exterior, a construction of an in-between condition, an inhabitable threshold, which becomes the main space of the project; the limits between the open and the content space merge to produce a single architectural entity.

The building respects the existing context, and understands that the vegetation and open air life are the real protagonists. The Tepoztlán Lounge is constructed of concrete, not just because it is an inexpensive and labor intensive material in Mexico and to minimize its maintenance, but also to expose its structural simplicity and neutrality next to the astonishing nature.

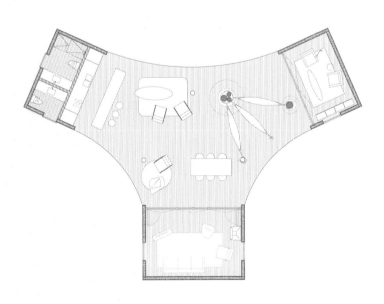

GETTING AROUND. TEPOZTLÁN, IS A SMALL TOWN NESTLED BETWEEN ROCKY CLIFFS LOCATED TO THE SOUTH OF MEXICO CITY, 50 KILOMETERS AWAY FROM THE VIBRANT METROPOLIS. WITH ITS WELL PRESERVED HISTORIC CENTER AND WILD COUNTRYSIDE, TEPOZTLÁN IS A TOWN OF LEGENDS AND DEEP CULTURAL ROOTS THAT HAS BEEN APPRECIATED BY WRITERS, POETS, ARTISTS AND MUSICIANS OVER MANY DECADES, TURNING IT INTO THEIR HOMETOWN OR WEEKEND RETREAT.

*Main view from the garden. Floor plan.
Detail of the roof.*

*Open kitchen with hammock.
Living and play area. Night view.*

GETTING AROUND. THE TERRITORY HOSTING THE ALBERGO DIFFUSO HAS A UNIQUE NATURAL BEAUTY, WHICH CAN BE ENJOYED THROUGH A WELL-DEVELOPED NETWORK OF NATURE-DISCOVERING ITINERARIES. THE CULTURAL LANDSCAPE HAS A MILLENNIAL HISTORY WHOSE VISIBLE TRACES GO BACK TO ANCIENT TIMES WHILE THE FOOD AND WINE PANORAMA DOES NOT JUST AIM AT MERE TOURISTIC GRATIFICATION. WINTER SPORTS ARE PARTICULARLY WELL ORGANIZED AND PERFECTLY FIT THE SURROUNDING MOUNTAINS AND THE LOCAL LONG HISTORY OF GREAT SPORT CHAMPIONS.

Exterior view of the house. Detail of the staircase. View of the living area with fireplace and big window.

Main view from the garden. View of the bedroom. Floor plan.

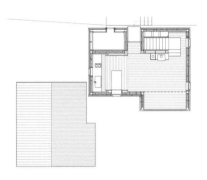

INFORMATION. ARCHITECTS>
CESCHIA E MENTIL ARCHITETTI
ASSOCIATI // 2014. HOUSE> 60 SQM //
2+1 GUESTS // 1 BEDROOM //
1 BATHROOM. ADDRESS> LOCALITÀ
FAAS, PALUZZA, ITALY.
WWW.ALBERGODIFFUSOPALUZZA.IT

Albergo Diffuso "La Marmote"

PALUZZA, ITALY

The building is distinguished by its simple and candid construction, without the superfluous elements of fake chalets. Its dynamic and emotional atmosphere is a result of the coating/cladding materials and formal elements such as the big window overlooking the alpine landscape. The house's interior design is intimately linked to the site's morphology. The cooking and dining area is a black space with a small window, the frameless big window is interactive, while a low window presents a constant glimpse of the outside, also sculpting a small wooden alcove, an intimate retreat for the night.

This integrated project was funded by the EU to restore and re-use the building's heritage to promote a new kind of tourism. The ambition is to no longer attract tourists with large accommodations but rather through small units that are widely spread across the territory. Tourists can enjoy a diversified, alternative, and economically approachable new kind of hospitality.

INFORMATION. ARCHITECTS> JARMUND / VIGSNÆS AS ARKITEKTER MNAL IN COLLABORATION WITH MOLE ARCHITECTS LTD// 2011. HOUSE> 250 SQM // 9 GUESTS // 4 BEDROOMS // 5 BATHROOMS. ADDRESS> THORPENESS, ENGLAND. WWW.LIVING-ARCHITECTURE.CO.UK/ THE-HOUSES/DUNE-HOUSE/OVERVIEW

The Dune House

THORPENESS, ENGLAND

To get a planning permission it was important to relate to the existing, typical, British seaside strip of houses. The roofscape and the bedroom floor somehow play with the formal presence of these buildings, and bring into mind romantic memories of holidays at bed- and breakfasts while traveling through England.

In contrast, the ground floor lacks any relationship to the architecture of the top floor. The living area and the terraces are set into the dunes in order to protect them from the strong winds, and open up equally in all directions to allow for wide views. The corners can be opened by sliding doors; this emphasizes the floating appearance of the top floor.

View of the kitchen. Exterior view. Night view of the house from the garden. Dining and living area with concrete fireplace.

View of the living room with large windows and wooden ceiling. Detail of one of the bedrooms. Floor plans. Main view at night.

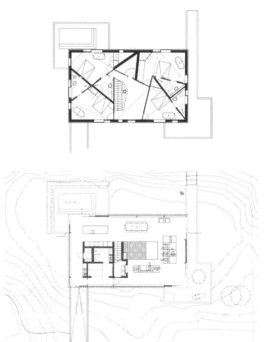

GETTING AROUND. THE DUNE HOUSE LIES JUST TO THE SOUTH OF THE PICTURESQUE VILLAGE OF THORPENESS IN SUFFOLK, ON AN IDYLLIC SPOT ON THE VERY EDGE OF THE SEA, NESTLED AMONG ROLLING DUNES. IT IS A HOLIDAY HOUSE FOR RENTAL THAT CAN ACCOMMODATE UP TO NINE PEOPLE. YOU CAN WALK OUT FROM THE LIVING ROOM DIRECTLY ONTO THE BEACH AND ENJOY EXTRAORDINARY PANORAMIC VIEWS OVER THE SEA FROM THE TERRACES, BEDROOMS, AND BATHROOMS ON THE UPPER FLOOR.

GETTING AROUND. SET IN THE SPECTACULAR VALLEY OF GUADALEST IN THE BENIMANTELL MUNICIPAL AREA, VIVOOD BLENDS INTO ITS NATURAL SURROUNDINGS, WHERE MEDITERRANEAN FOREST MERGES WITH TERRACED MOUNTAINSIDES DATING TO THE MUSLIM ERA. THIS IS THE IDEAL BASE FOR EXPLORING INTERESTING SITES SUCH AS GUADALEST RESERVOIR, THE AITANA AND XORTÀ MOUNTAIN RANGES, VIEWS OF BENIMANTELL, BENIARDÀ, ABDET, GUADALEST; ARCHAEOLOGICAL SITES, AND EXCEPTIONAL SCENERY AND PLANT LIFE.

Views from the suites to Guadalest Valley. Private terrace and heated jacuzzi. View of the cabin from below. Suite with floor-to-ceiling windows to enjoy views.

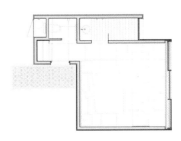

INFORMATION. ARCHITECTS>
DANIEL MAYO, AGUSTÍN MARÍ,
PABLO VÁZQUEZ, MARINA PUCHE.
DESIGNER> AMANDA GLEZ // 2015.
HOTEL> 27 SQM EACH SUITE //
2 GUESTS PER SUITE // 25 SUITES //
25 BATHROOMS. ADDRESS> VALLE DE
GUADALEST, BENIMANTELL, SPAIN.
WWW.VIVOOD.COM

VIVOOD Landscape Hotels

VALLE DE GUADALEST, SPAIN

VIVOOD Landscape Hotels is a new hotel chain, designed and managed by architects with a passion for creating spaces offering a unique experience to their guests. It consists of 25 independent suites, a restaurant and lounge bar, a panoramic swimming pool, terraces, and outdoor hot tubs, nestled in the heart of nature. Travelers can find peace and quiet in exclusive surroundings.

VIVOOD is based on the basic premise of the landscape hotel concept. Modules are positioned on the land without changing its topography, and anchored to the ground using an innocuous, reversible foundation system. Each unit is independent and separate to ensure privacy. The project used sustainable materials and techniques and blends beautifully into the environment.

The main building materials used are wood and black Viroc. The entire hotel is installed with low consumption ambient lighting that guide guests around the site at night but have no environmental impact and cause no light pollution.

INFORMATION. ARCHITECT>
EVOLUTION DESIGN // 2015. HOUSE>
141 SQM // 7 GUESTS // 4 BEDROOMS
// 3 BATHROOMS. ADDRESS> FOREST
IN TEESDALE, ENGLAND.
WWW.CHAPEL-ON-THE-HILL.COM

The Chapel on the Hill

FOREST IN TEESDALE, ENGLAND

After standing derelict for more than 40 years, this former Methodist chapel has been brought back to life and turned into a boutique holiday cottage. Located away from it all in a rural English countryside with picturesque views to the rolling hills nearby, Chapel is a perfect location for tranquil and relaxing holidays.

The main aim of the conversion was to retain the original characteristics of this chapel: the tall Gothic windows, which flood the space with daylight and offer dramatic views of the countryside and the weather outside, and the main congregation hall, which has been turned into a spacious kitchen and homely living room with a log burner – the very heart of this holiday home.

The new mezzanine floor above has been inserted without obstructing the tall Gothic windows, offering enough of space for two master bedrooms with en-suits and another single bedroom in-between.

Kitchen with dining area. Main entrance of the house. Side view from the garden. Living room with stairs seen from the kitchen.

Main view of the old chapel. Floor plans. View of the kitchen with wooden beams and Gothic windows.

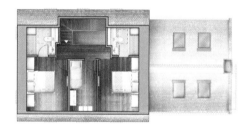

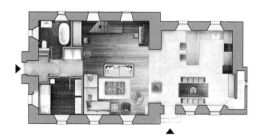

GETTING AROUND. CHAPEL IS SET IN THE BEST WALKING AREA OF THE BEAUTIFUL NORTH PENNINES WITH MANY STUNNING FOOTPATHS STARTING AT ITS DOORSTEP. THE PENNINE WAY (A 429-KILOMETER LONG NATIONAL TRAIL) OFFERS BREATH-TAKING VIEWS AND A GREAT WALKING EXPERIENCE. THE MAJESTIC HIGH FORCE WATERFALL CAN BE REACHED WITHIN HALF AN HOUR. BARNARD CASTLE HAS MANY TEAROOMS AND BOUTIQUES. THE BOWES MUSEUM HOUSES INTERNATIONALLY RENOWNED COLLECTIONS OF EUROPEAN ARTS SPANNING FIVE CENTURIES.

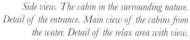

Side view. The cabin in the surrounding nature.
Detail of the entrance. Main view of the cabins from
the water. Detail of the relax area with view.

Manshausen Island Resort

MANSHAUSEN ISLAND, NORWAY

Manshausen Island is situated off the coast of Northern Norway. The resort was planned and laid out in consideration of the Island's topography and the two main existing structures – the old farmhouse and the stone quays.

The farmhouse was carefully restored and contains a dining area and library. The cabins are placed on the stone quays or on the rocky formations above. The positioning and orientation of all the cabins is based on their individual panoramic views and privacy of the guests.

The cabins are designed to offer shelter and comfort while at the same time underlining the dramatic experience of the elements outside;

the sea, landscape, changing lights, weather and different seasons.

They offer ample space for luggage and clothing/equipment, a comfortable bathroom and a kitchen/dining area. The main bedroom is fully glazed to allow experience of the outside elements, while being comfortably sheltered inside.

INFORMATION. ARCHITECTS>
SNORRE STINESSEN / STINESSEN
ARKITEKTUR AS // 2015. 4 CABINS>
33 SQM EACH CABIN // 4–5 GUESTS
PER CABIN // 2 BEDROOMS EACH //
1 BATHROOM EACH. ADDRESS>
MANSHAUSEN ISLAND, STEIGEN,
NORWAY.
WWW.MANSHAUSEN.NO

GETTING AROUND. MANSHAUSEN OFFERS A WIDE VARIETY OF ACTIVITIES IN ITS VICINITY, INCLUDING KAYAKING, SAILING, DIVING, SNORKELING, FISHING, BOAT RENTAL, BOAT TOURS IN THE ARCHIPELAGO, SEA EAGLE SPOTTING, CAVE EXPLORATION, CLIMBING, MOUNTAIN TREKKING, AND OFF-PISTE SKIING.

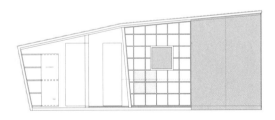

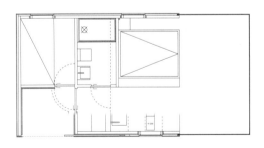

General view of the cabins. Floor plan and section. View of the surronding landscape.

The sleeping area. Detail of the side façade with large windows. Exterior view of the cabin.

INFORMATION. ARCHITECTS>
CADAVAL & SOLÀ-MORALES // 2006.
HOUSE> 350 SQM // 8 GUESTS //
3 BEDROOMS // 2 BATHROOMS.
ADDRESS> PUERTO ESCONDIDO,
OAXACA, MEXICO.
WWW.AIRBNB.DE/ROOMS/498808

TDA House

PUERTO ESCONDIDO, MEXICO

Located on the Pacific coast of Mexico this low-cost/low-maintenance house for extreme weather is suitable for any number of inhabitants. It has flexible uses and configurations, optionally completely open to the exterior or closed in on itself. Almost all remnant materials of the construction process were recycled and used in its design.

Due to the local high temperatures, salpeter, and unskilled labor, the house was made of concrete with its structural capabilities and resistance to extreme conditions.

The house consists of three elements that are defined for three different functions: a tower volume whose opacity is interrupted at strategic points until it is completely open and nothing blocks its views over the ocean. A second bedroom volume suspended over the water and the wild flowers of the garden; and a third element built as a wide, high, fresh central space, which distributes and channels the different activities of the house.

View of the house. View of the living area. Detail of the roof terrace with red hammocks. Exterior view.

Main view of the swimming pool and house with large openings. Floor plans. The silhouette of the house with the two big cantilevers.

GETTING AROUND. THE ULTIMATE ARCHITECTURAL AIM OF THE PROJECT IS TO OFFER LIFE IN COMMUNITY, IN THE OPEN AIR; A LIVING PORTRAIT OF THE VITAL MEXICAN UTOPIA, THAT IS, A WORLD OF HARMONY, COLOR, AND NATURE, A REFLECTION OF THE ROCKING OF THE HAMMOCKS AND THE PLEASURE OF THE DOLCE FAR NIENTE.

GETTING AROUND. LOCATED IN THE IMMEDIATE VICINITY, THE VISITOR CENTER OF THE NATURE PARK HOCHMOOR SCHREMS OFFERS A FASCINATING INSIGHT INTO THE LANDSCAPE OF THE WALDVIERTEL'S PONDS AND BOGS. CLIMBING UP 108 STAIRS ON THE HIMMELSLEITER, VISITORS CAN ENJOY A PANORAMIC VIEW AT 20 METERS HEIGHT. THE ART MUSEUM AND IDEA DESIGN CENTER, MUD BATH, SCHREMS BREWERY, CHEESE MAKING WORKSHOP, THE SALINE BATH, MONASTERIES AND ABBEYS, HIKING AND BIKING PATHS, ARE JUST A FEW OF THE LOCAL ATTRACTIONS.

The bright sleeping and living area of one of the three treehouses. Detail of the large covered balcony. View from the entrance walkway. The tower from below.

Exterior night view of the lodges from the forest.
Floor plans.

INFORMATION. ARCHITECT>
BAUMRAUM, ANDREAS WENNING //
2014. CABINS> 18 SQM EACH (THE
HOUSES), 30 SQM (THE TOWER) //
8 GUESTS // 1 BEDROOM EACH //
1 BATHROOM EACH. ADDRESS>
MOORBADSTRASSE 6, SCHREMS,
AUSTRIA.
WWW.BAUMHAUS-LODGE.AT

Baumhaus Lodge Schrems

SCHREMS, AUSTRIA

The Baumhaus Lodge was constructed next to a small granite quarry pond. A ravine path, steep rock cliffs, a pond, small ground depressions, moss-covered rock walls and various trees are just some of the areas awaiting exploration.

The lodge currently consists of three treehouses at heights ranging from 5 to 17 meters above ground. Two additional treehouses near the lake are almost completed. The house near the wall, the house near the base and the cliff houses accommodate two persons each, and the tower house offers room for four people across two levels.

Sitting on galvanized steel profiles, the treehouses are constructed out of solid timber plates and wood fiber insulating boards with brushed aluminum façades. The translucent cladding of the tower house consists of rough-sawn square-shaped larch wood.

INFORMATION. ARCHITECTS>
Z-LEVEL ARCHITECTURE, ELENA
ZERVOUDAKIS // 2011. TOWER
HOUSE> 150 SQM // 8–10 GUESTS //
3 BEDROOMS // 2 BATHROOMS.
ADDRESS> EXO NYFI, MANI,
PELOPONNESE, GREECE.
WWW.MAINA.GR

*Kitchen and dining area. Outdoor seating between the
towers. Dining area and kitchen feature cement floor
and wooden roof, stone walls and pastel earthy colors.*

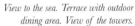
View to the sea. Terrace with outdoor dining area. View of the towers.

Maina

MANI, PELOPONNESE,
GREECE

Nestled in a quaint village of traditional stone towers in Eastern Mani, this hillside house looks out over olive groves and the sea which is just a five minute drive away. Originally an abandoned megalithic 18th-century two-story building, the house is surrounded by a garden with olive trees, carob trees and prickly pears, even a cave, offering an ideal place for privacy and relaxation. To the east, the yard abuts a 16th-century tower, and just below there is a Byzantine chapel with frescoes.

The stone tower house was renovated and expanded by architect Elena Zervoudakis, preserving the building's traditional elements and combining them with minimalist interiors for a sense of serenity and originality. The 150-square-meter house is built into the slope and thus evolves over three levels, each with access to the garden and verandas.

Its recent conversion to an ecologically-minded holiday villa using local materials and techniques, rainwater harvesting and eco-friendly waste disposal system for irrigation aspires to leave a light footprint on the long history of the building.

*Kitchen in the vault. Family bedroom on ground level.
Bedroom on third level. Wooden staircase leading to
the second level. Plan of the third level.*

GETTING AROUND. MAINA IS THE
PERFECT STARTING POINT TO DIS-
COVER THE NATURAL BEAUTY OF
MANI AND ITS CULTURAL WEALTH.
IT IS A UNIQUE BLEND OF MOUN-
TAINOUS LANDSCAPE AND COAST-
LINE WITH BEACHES, SMALL COVES,
BYZANTINE CHURCHES, AND TOWER
HOUSES. THE PATH TO THE ANCIENT
CITY OF AIGILA AND THE MONASTERY
OF KROUNOS PASSES RIGHT IN FRONT
OF THE HOUSE. MOUNT TAYGETOS
IS ALSO IN THE VICINITY. ACTIVITIES
INCLUDE HORSEBACK RIDING, HAR-
VESTING OLIVES, AND SAMPLING THE
WONDERFUL CUISINE.

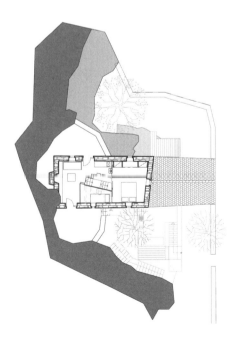

INFORMATION. ARCHITECT> BUREAU A // 2014. CABIN> 4 SQM // 1 GUEST // 1 ROOM. ADDRESS> LES RUINETTES, VERBIER, SWITZERLAND. WWW.3-DFOUNDATION.COM

Main view of the shelter in the surrounding lanscape.
Detail of the single window of the tiny cabin.

Antoine

LES RUINETTES, SWITZERLAND

Switzerland has a long tradition of observing the Alps, living with them, hiding inside them. The awe and the anxiety that this monumental landscape evokes is reflected in the writings of Charles-Ferdinand Ramuz, one of the most important Swiss writers. His novel Derborence describes the slide of a massive piece rock that covered the pastures of the valley of Lizerne in 1714. Antoine, the main character, survives seven weeks under the rocks before he manages to return to his village and his life.

Antoine is an alpine shelter inside a projecting concrete boulder, a precarious "mere subsistence" where one can freely enter and hide. Containing only the very basic architectural elements for one person – fireplace, bed, table, stool, window it bears an element of risk as the boulder literally hangs on the rock fall field.

Antoine was commissioned by the artist residency Verbier 3d Foundation. It was built in the village and transported to the high-altitude sculpture park.

GETTING AROUND. ANTOINE IS A TRIBUTE TO THE ALPINE EXPERIENCE AND TO THE WRITER. THE SMALL WOODEN CABIN IS HIDDEN INSIDE A PROJECTED CONCRETE ROCK. REFERRING TO THE LONG SWISS TRADITION OF HIDDEN BUNKERS, THE PROJECT INTEGRATES THE HIGHLY URBANIZED LANDSCAPE OF THE ALPS. ALREADY DESCRIBED BY THE FRENCH PHILOSOPHER PAUL VIRILIO IN 1975, THE ARCHITECTS WERE FASCINATED WITH MILITARY ARCHITECTURE CONDUCTED BY PRINCIPLES OF CAMOUFLAGE.

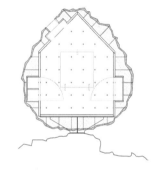

Winter view of the shelter. The interior of the cabin with a wood burner and basic fold-down panels as table, bed and seating. Section. The wooden heart of the cabin before being enclosed in the concrete.

Casa no Tempo

ALENTEJO, PORTUGAL

Casa no Tempo has been owned by the same family for many years. The founder's will was that the next generations take care of it. The current owners aim even higher, connecting the past with the future, erasing the marks of time to create a peaceful and timeless place.

The renovation was supervised by architect Manuel Aires Mateus. The main concern was to open the house up to the vast property and welcome nature through large windows in every room.

The garden consists of one thousand acres of cork trees, pastures, wild fields, two dams, five ponds, streams and brooks. Here and there, timeless granite stones jut out of the green and stand by the trees

or water as random natural signposts, inviting guests to explore and journey through the welcoming flat land. A 400-square-meter swimming pool intercepts the pasture with its modern design and sand colored plaster.

INFORMATION. ARCHITECT>
MANUEL AIRES MATEUS // 2014.
HOUSE> 340 SQM // 8 GUESTS //
4 BEDROOMS // 4 BATHROOMS.
ADDRESS> HERDADE DO CARVALHO,
SABUGUEIRO ARRAIOLOS, PORTUGAL.
WWW.CASANOTEMPO.COM

GETTING AROUND. CASA NO TEMPO IS SITUATED 1 HOUR SOUTH OF LISBON IN MONTEMOR O NOVO, ALENTEJO, CLOSE TO THE WORLD HERITAGE SITE ÉVORA CITY IN A UNIQUE LANDSCAPE OF GOLDEN PLAINS. VISITORS CAN ENJOY MANY ACTIVITIES: SWIMMING, FISHING, CYCLING, OR HORSEBACK RIDING. THERE ARE COWS, SHEEP, GOATS, CHICKENS, DUCKS, PEACOCKS, DOGS. OR THEY CAN ENJOY PICNICS AND SAMPLE FARM PRODUCTS SUCH AS HONEY, GOAT CHEESE, ORGANIC MEAT AND EGGS, OLIVE OIL, CORK, JAMS, AND VEGETABLES.

Side view. Interior view of the bright living area.
View of the swimming pool.

Sleeping area.
View of the kitchen with dining area.
Main entrance paved with local clay blocks,
like all floors of the house.

INFORMATION. ARCHITECT> GRACIASTUDIO // 2011. HOTEL> 20 ROOMS OF 25 SQM EACH // 2 GUESTS PER ROOM // 1 BEDROOM EACH // 1 BATHROOM EACH. ADDRESS> VALLE DE GUADALUPE, ENSENADA, MEXICO. WWW.HOTELENDEMICO.COM

Encuentro Guadalupe

VALLE DE GUADALUPE, MEXICO

Located in Valle de Guadalupe "Mexico's Wine Country", Baja California, Encuentro Guadalupe is a 94-hectare tourism development, comprised of a winery, hotel, and residential area. It has its own vineyards, as well as an event and tasting area, along with restaurants for its guests and general public all year long.

The hotel is formed by a set of twenty independent rooms of twenty-five square meters each. One of the principal premises was not to interfere directly with the land, as part of the philosophy of the project is to respect nature in every possible way. The use of steel gives the design a clean structure with the material used to elevate the skeleton of the rooms to avoid contact with the soil.

For the exterior cover Corten steel was used, which changes its color over time, achieving harmony between the environment and the building.

View of the panoramic swimming pool. Main view of the cabin from below. The cabins nestled in the surrounding nature. Back view from the private terrace.

View of the bedroom and the private terrace. General view of the cabins. Interior view of the room. Floor plan. Sleeping area with large panoramic window.

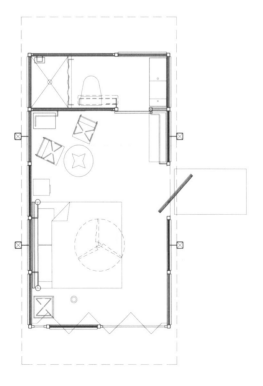

GETTING AROUND. THE DESIGN OF THE ROOMS IS THAT OF A "DELUXE" CAMPING HOUSE, COVERING THE GUEST'S BASIC NEEDS, PROVIDING CONTACT WITH NATURE AND THE ENVIRONMENT. ENCUENTRO GUADALUPE IS A PLACE WITH UNIQUE CHARACTERISTICS, PRESENTING THE OPPORTUNITY TO APPRECIATE THE LANDSCAPE IN AN UNPARALLELED WAY, COUPLED WITH UNDERSTATED ARCHITECTURE THAT PROVIDES THE USERS WITH THE BASICS DURING THEIR STAY: AN EXPERIENCE OF CONVENIENCE AND PROTECTION.

GETTING AROUND. THE TWO TREEHOUSES ARE SITUATED ON A 650-SQUARE-METER GARDEN PLOT WITH MANY TREES THAT IMMEDIATELY BORDERS ON A FOREST. THE STRAIGHT LINE DISTANCE TO THE SWIMMING LAKE KRUMME LANKE, WHICH BORDERS THE SCHLACHTENSEE LAKE, IS 300 METERS BEHIND THE HOUSE. THE URBAN TREEHOUSE IS A FAMILY PROJECT, INITIATED BY A GRANDSON AND GRANDFATHER. IT IS AN EXPERIMENT AND A RESEARCH PROJECT FOR NEW, EXPERIMENTAL, NATURAL CONSTRUCTION AND LIVING. IT IS INTENDED TO SERVE AS AN INSPIRATION AND SOURCE OF ENERGY TO FRIENDS, GUESTS, STUDENTS, AND FANS OF ARCHITECTURE.

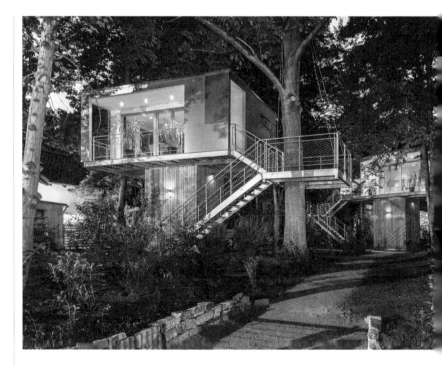

Main view of the treehouse. Detail of the kitchen.
Interior view of the kitchen and dining area.
Exterior night view.

Living and dining area with large windows.
View from below. Cross section.

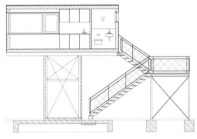

INFORMATION. ARCHITECT>
BAUMRAUM, ANDREAS WENNING //
2014. TREEHOUSE> 24 SQM EACH //
2 GUESTS // 1 BEDROOM // 1 BATH-
ROOM. ADDRESS> QUERMATENWEG
23, BERLIN, GERMANY.
WWW.URBAN-TREEHOUSE-BERLIN.
COM

Urban Treehouse

BERLIN, GERMANY

The Urban Treehouse stands aloof inspiring visitors to pause and ponder, to change their perspective and to be rejuvenated. Standing 4-meter high and offering twenty-four meters of space, the treehouses contain everything required by an exclusive studio above the ground: living room and bedroom, fully equipped kitchen, bathroom with rain shower, and a covered terrace.

The solid wood structure ensures a natural climate, combined with modern designer furniture it offers a modern and comfortable atmosphere. The houses were deliberately placed in a residential area located at the border of the city and nature.

Residents can live a normal everyday life – going shopping, to restaurants or pubs, parking the car on the street and greeting the neighbors. At the same time, they reside in the middle of nature, at eye level with tree tops, birds, and the sky over Berlin.

Baix de S'Era

MALLORCA, SPAIN

Baix de S'Era is a wonderful finca in Alaró, in the central part of the island of Mallorca. The unimpeded view of the impressive Tramuntana mountain range invites friends and families to enjoy an unforgettable holiday.

Available for rent year-round, the finca offers everything vacationers may desire, from a private pool via a beautiful designer kitchen up to a generously proportioned living area. Across approximately 230 square meters there are six rooms – three bedrooms, a multi-function room (which can also be used as a bedroom for two), a living room and a kitchen, along with three bathrooms, WC, housekeeping room and garage.

Directly next to the house there is a 3.5 x 11-meter fresh water pool and a huge 170-square-meter terrace, of which 45 square meters are located between the housekeeping and living sections protected from sun and wind.

View from the garden of the rear side of the house. The main entrance, with large wooden and glass door. Main view at night.

INFORMATION. ARCHITECT> JAUME COLOM, CLM ARQUITECTURA, ALARÓ // 2015. HOUSE> 230 SQM // 8 GUESTS // 4 BEDROOMS // 3 BATHROOMS. ADDRESS> SON POL, ALARÓ, MALLORCA, SPAIN. WWW.BAIXDESERA.DE

GETTING AROUND. THE REGION OFFERS MANY OPPORTUNITIES FOR SPORTS SUCH AS BICYCLING, HIKING, JOGGING, SWIMMING, SAILING, SURFING, TENNIS, HORSEBACK RIDING AND PLAYING GOLF. THE MAIN POINT OF INTEREST IN ALARÓ IS THE CASTELL D'ALARÓ LOCATED 824 METERS ABOVE SEA LEVEL. AFTER CLIMBING UP TO IT, VISITORS ARE REWARDED WITH A BREATHTAKING PANORAMIC VIEW OF MALLORCA.

View of terrace with pool, relax and outdoor dining area. Ground floor plan. Detail of the entrance, with large window and sitting area.

*View of the living room.
One of the bedrooms with private bathroom. The kitchen with dining area for eight people.*

INFORMATION. ARCHITECT> LONGO
+ ROLDÁN ARQUITECTOS // 2011.
HOUSE> 484.40 SQM // 10 GUESTS //
5 BEDROOMS // 5 BATHROOMS.
ADDRESS> LA PEREDA, LLANES,
ASTURIAS, SPAIN.
WWW.CAEACLAVELES.COM

CAEa-CLAVELES

ASTURIAS, SPAIN

The topography of the site, its orientation and mountain views of Cuera were the starting points for the design of an artist's residence/studio + countryside B&B in the village of Llanes, Spain. The project takes advantage of a loophole in the law – which requires regional pitched roofs of curved ceramic tile – to propose a building that is more integrated with the natural beauty of the area than with the built environment around it.

The hill was removed to accommodate a single green roof over the entire complex, diluting the boundaries between the natural and the built. A curved wall leads from the road into the building, gaining altitude to become a load bearing wall for the concrete deck that separates the private residence/studio of the artist from the small B&B. This central wall, massive and powerful to ensure the privacy of both areas, contrasts with the façades of the housing area and the B&B, which are lighter and visually permeable. The roof slopes to merge with the ground not only to integrate the building into the environment and naturally minimize the height above the ground but also to maximize energy savings.

View of the living area. Detail of the roof garden. General view. Exterior view of the living room and the organic form of the roof.

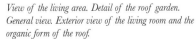

Detail of the entrance and the different materials of the façade. View of the organic volume from the roof. Floor plan.

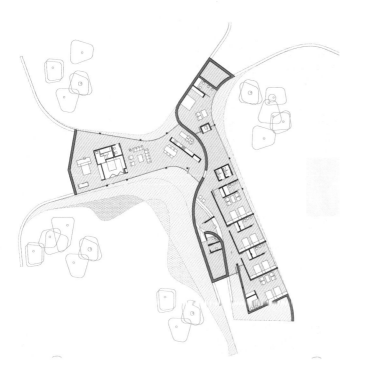

GETTING AROUND. CAEACLAVELES IS ALL ABOUT GEOGRAPHY. IMMERSED INTO THE PROTECTED LANDSCAPE OF THE EASTERN COAST OF CUERA, AT LA PEREDA, BETWEEN THE CANTABRIAN SEA AND THE "PICOS DE EUROPA", IT OFFERS 48 KILOMETERS OF COASTLINE AND 38 BEACHES OF FINE SAND AND EXTREME BEAUTY. THE CONTRASTING LANDSCAPE IS INTIMATE, PRESERVED, WILD, SOMETIMES HIDDEN IN SMALL FJORDS, OR OPEN IN BEAUTIFUL COVES. BEACHES INCLUDE TORIMBIA, TORANDA, BALLOTA, POO, SAN MARTÍN, OR BUELNA.

Exterior detail of the house, symbiotic with the environment and linked to the characteristic features of the area. Interior view.

INFORMATION. ARCHITECTS>
DESIGNBUILDBLUFF AT THE UNIVERSI-
TY OF UTAH IN COLLABORATION WITH
COLORADOBUILDINGWORKSHOP AT
THE UNIVERSITY OF COLORADO,
DENVER // 2014. CABIN> 27 SQM //
4–6 GUESTS // 1 BEDROOM //
1 BATHROOM. ADDRESS> NAVAJO
NATION, RED MESA, ARIZONA, USA.
WWW.DESIGNBUILDBLUFF.ORG

Mexican Water Cabins

NAVAJO NATION, USA

Set in the desert of south-eastern Utah, the Mexican Water Cabins are influenced by the landscape and distant views of the Blue Mountains and Monument Valley. Two sibling cubes (Sunrise and Sunset) were designed to contrast one another. One rests on the landscape while the other emerges from it.

Each cabin establishes its own identity while simultaneously evoking the same language. Entering the Sunset Cabin requires a journey through the patio first, while the journey to Sunrise Cabin is through the building and out toward the cantilevered patio. Both patios, located on the northern side of the cabins, provide shade in the summer and are clad in reclaimed barn wood.

Concrete floors, sinks, and counters contrast the reclaimed barn wood on the interior walls and bedrooms while the weathered steel exterior resembles the red sand of the landscape. Apertures in both cabins frame views of the surrounding natural environment: the sand, mountains, and sky.

View of the cabins in the surroundings nature. Sleeping area and living space. View of the patio with fireplace. The two cabins nestled in the Navajo reserve.

Detail of the entrance. Sleeping area. View of the two cabins. Floor plans. View of the interior space, covered by reclaimed barn wood.

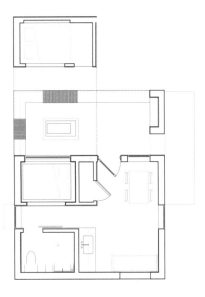

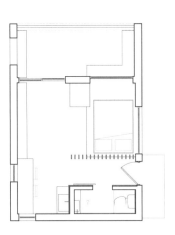

GETTING AROUND. THE AREA IS HOME TO THE REMAINS OF THE PREHISTORIC ANASAZI INDIAN CIVILIZATION, AS WELL AS PICTURESQUE MONUMENT VALLEY AND IS WITHIN DRIVING DISTANCE OF A NUMBER OF NATIONAL PARKS. THE CLOSEST PARKS INCLUDE HOVENWEEP, MESA VERDE, NATURAL BRIDGES, CANYONLANDS, ARCHES, AND NAVAJO NATIONAL MONUMENT.

View of the bright sleeping area. Detail of the modern design furnitures.

INFORMATION. ARCHITECT> STUDIO NR. 7 // 2014. APARTMENT> 25 SQM // 4 GUESTS // 2 BEDROOMS // 1 BATHROOM. ADDRESS> KLEINE BLEEKSTRAAT 7, EINDHOVEN, THE NETHERLANDS. WWW.STUDIONR7.NL

Bed and Breakfast Studio Nr. 7

EINDHOVEN, THE NETHERLANDS

Studio Nr. 7 is a unique Bed & Breakfast located in the heart of the design city of Eindhoven, designed and built by the owners.

"The whole world comes into our house by way of our guest rooms, bringing different stories and outlooks, which inspire us in the writing of our own story. During our travels across South America, we asked ourselves what our perfect Bed & Breakfast would look like. We stayed at so many places and met so many people, each with his or her own story. We saw the importance of them all, and realized that all these different views kept our minds open.

So for us, an open mind is the key to good design, but also to a comfortable and carefree stay.

This attitude is the common approach in our Bed & Breakfast. We think it's important to be professional, but never to forget about the personal touch!"

GETTING AROUND. STUDIO NR. 7 IS LOCATED IN THE CENTER OF EINDHOVEN. THE PHILIPS CORPORATION WAS FOUNDED IN EINDHOVEN, WHICH INFLUENCED THE CITY EVER SINCE. IT IS A CITY BURSTING WITH ENERGY, INNOVATION AND TECHNOLOGY, AND MOST IMPORTANTLY: IT'S THE DESIGN CAPITAL OF THE NETHERLANDS. MANY EVENTS ARE ORGANIZED YEAR-ROUND, INCLUDING THE "DUTCH DESIGN WEEK" AND "GLOW EINDHOVEN."
EINDHOVEN IS ALSO SURROUNDED BY NATURE THAT CAN BE EXPLORED USING THE EXTENSIVE NETWORK OF HIKING AND BICYCLE PATHS.

Detail of the sitting niche in the sleeping area.
View of the top terrace. Floor plans.

119

INFORMATION. ARCHITECTS>
MATTEO THUN & PARTNERS SRL,
MILAN AND STEIN, HEMMES & WIRTZ,
KASEL // 2013. VINEYARD COTTAGE>
26 SQM EACH COTTAGE // 2 GUESTS
EACH // 1 BEDROOM EACH //
1 BATHROOM EACH. ADDRESS>
KIRCHENWEG 9, LONGUICH,
GERMANY.
WWW.LONGEN-SCHLOEDER.DE

Winery Longen-Schlöder

LONGUICH, GERMANY

The Longen family has been cultivating vineyards on the slopes of the Mosel valley in harmony with nature for many generations. Now they offer an idyll: an orchard surrounded by orchards where guests can experience wine and fruit growing, rural structures, and life in harmony with nature. This philosophy is expressed in the new vintner houses, the expanded restaurant (seating 70), and the new main building.

The Longens' guests reside in the midst of fruit, walnut, linden and chestnuts trees in 20 small stone houses made of local shale. Each of the houses, some of which can be combined into "family houses", features a small wooden terrace and a private garden. These are basically designed as classic kitchen or herbal gardens and visitors can choose the desired garden along with the house. The design of the 20-square-meter shale houses is bright, clear and pure. The furnishings predominately feature timber, the color white, as well as natural fabrics and materials.

Main view of the cottage by night. View from the bedroom to the private garden. Common dining area. View of the cottages from the garden.

*Exterior night view. Dressing table inside the bedroom.
Detail of the wooden entrance door. Section, floor
plan, front and back view. View of the sleeping area.*

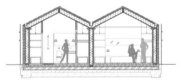

GETTING AROUND. THE LONGEN-SCHLÖDER WINERY HAS BEEN OPERATED BY THE SAME FAMILY FOR MANY GENERATIONS. ITS VARIOUS HILLS AND SLOPES ARE EXCELLENTLY SUITED FOR GROWING A VARIETY OF WHITE AND RED WINES. THE AREA IS ALSO RICH IN HISTORIC AND CULTURAL SITES, SUCH AS TRIER WITH ITS ROMAN ARTIFACTS, LUXEMBOURG, THE ROMANTIC VILLAGE OF BERNKASTEL-KUES, AND THE EXTENDED MOSEL VALLEY WITH ITS COUNTLESS HIKING AND BIKING PATHS AND NEARBY SHALE MINE.

GETTING AROUND. FLOATWING ALLOWS LIVING ON THE SURFACE OF A LAKE IN ULTIMATE SECURITY AND COMFORT, MOVING AT A MODERATE SPEED OF 4 KNOTS, CHOOSING A NEW LOCATION FOR ANCHORING AT WILL EVERY DAY, AND SETTING OUT ON A NUMBER OF WATER SPORTS, OR SIMPLY ENJOYING THE WORLD'S BEST PLACE TO SUNBATH, TO SEE THE STARS, AND TO REST.

General view of the floating house. The living area completely surrounded by windows.

INFORMATION. ARCHITECT> FRIDAY // 2015. FLOATING HOUSE> FROM 28 SQM TO 52 SQM // 2–6 GUESTS // FROM 0 TO 3 DOUBLE BEDROOMS // 1 BATHROOM. ADDRESS> ALL OVER THE WORLD. WWW.GOFRIDAY.EU

View of the dining room with a small cooking area. Detail of the bedroom. Floor plans.

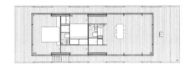

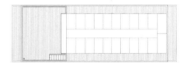

FloatWing

ALL OVER THE WORLD

FloatWing offers the opportunity for residents of big cities to periodically escape the hustle and bustle of everyday life, to engage in leisure activities and responsible fun, and to enjoy nature without giving up a good deal of comfort.

The approach was to combine elements of mountain resorts, lighthouses, isolated mills and forest huts, to add mobility and adopt the principles of prefabrication, modularity, energy autonomy and environmental sustainability.

The result is a product that is highly innovative in many respects: a floating house that produces 30 to 90 percent of the energy it requires over the annual cycle itself and reduces the organic load of its wastewater by up to 100 percent. It allows freedom of movement as it glides over the water surface, and is the ideally setting for water sports or pure relaxation.

INFORMATION. ARCHITECTS>
LAKONIS ARCHITEKTEN // 2014.
HOUSE> 310 SQM // 5–8 GUESTS //
7 BEDROOMS // 4 BATHROOMS.
ADDRESS> SEESTRASSE 31,
TRAUNKIRCHEN, AUSTRIA.
WWW.TRAUNSEE31.AT

*Chill area with a great lake view.
Dining area. Exterior view of the house
with terraces at different levels.*

SEE 31

TRAUNKIRCHEN, AUSTRIA

In the summer of 2014 a special vacation destination was created in the Salzkammergut area of Austria. It consists of two wooden houses with a picturesque beach on the shore of Traunsee, surrounded by flower fields, trees and mountains.

Structured to resemble the dispersed settlements of the region, the first house offers 150 square meters of space for up to eight persons, and the second cube offers two 80-square-meter apartments, each of which can accommodate up to eight persons. A generously proportioned living/cooking/dining area is at the center of each house.

The design focused on modern comfort, limited, mostly untreated, materials, and an unlimited view across the lake. Noble surface finishes of local materials – larch wood, felt, stone, and glass, in addition to high-quality furnishings dominate the ambiance. The compact bedrooms in combination with the private sauna and fireplace constitute a perfect relaxation zone.

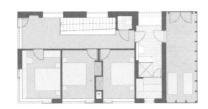

GETTING AROUND. TRAUNKIRCHEN IS A PICTURESQUE VACATION RESORT IN THE SALZKAMMERGUT REGION DOMINATED BY THE IMPRESSIVE BACKDROP OF TRAUNSTEIN. OFFERING A UNIQUE MIX OF CULTURE AND NATURE, THE CLEARLY MARKED HIKING TRAILS INVITE VISITORS TO EXPLORE AND DISCOVER THE VARIED LANDSCAPE WITH ITS MANY HIGHLIGHTS, INCLUDING FLOWSTONE CAVES AND WATER SPORTS ON THE TRAUNSEE. IN WINTER, THERE ARE ALSO MANY SKI RESORTS IN THE VICINITY.

Main view of the two buildings. Ground and first floor plans. Detail of the bathroom and the finnish sauna. Winter view of the house and the frozen lake.

View of the kitchen.
Detail of the glass corner on the ground floor.

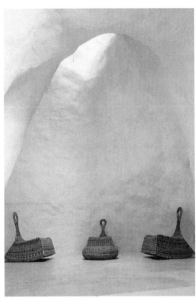

GETTING AROUND. THE AREA IS
CHARACTERIZED BY STONE BUILD-
INGS, OLIVE TREES, AND CAROBS.
NEARBY TOWNS INCLUDE RAGUSA,
CALTAGIRONE, SCICLI, ISPICA, NOTO,
SIRACUSA, THE BEACHES OF SAMP-
IERI, MARINA DI MODICA, MARINA
DI RAGUSA, THE NATURAL RESERVE
OF VENDICARI, MARZAMEMI, AND
KAMARINA. THE AREA IS FAMOUS FOR
ITS WINE AND CUISINE. MALTA CAN BE
REACHED BY HYDROFOIL.
ACTIVITIES INCLUDE WIND AND KITE
SURFING, SAILING, HORSEBACK RID-
ING, FISHING AND LIGHT FLYING.

One of the bedrooms with a tipycal stone wall.
View of the breakfast room. The garden
with a view of the city.

INFORMATION. ARCHITECTS>
VIVIANA HADDAD AND MARCO
GIUNTA // 2012. BOUTIQUE HOTEL>
500 SQM // 30 GUESTS // 10
BEDROOMS // 10 BATHROOMS.
ADDRESS> MODICA, SICILY, ITALY.
WWW.CASATALIA.IT

View of the bedroom with lime plasters. Detail of the polychrom tiled wall in the bedroom. Site plan.

Casa Talía

MODICA, ITALY

Talía is a fascinating place, an island on an island, where harmony is the main protagonist, thanks to the meticulous restoration by the two owners, Marco Giunta and Viviana Haddad – a married couple of architects from Milan who decided to live in Modica choosing slow living over city life.

The restoration of the rooms was inspired by the unique features of Arabic houses in the Medina area, providing peaceful spaces in the heart of a busy town. Like a Moroccan riad, rooms in Talía are independent, but all are connected facing the central garden, which is an important spatial element offering a place for encounters.

Great attention was given to the careful choice of materials, which are natural, ecological, and, above all, typical of the Sicilian tradition: stone walls, lime plastering, cane roofs, stone, and polychrome tiled floors.

INFORMATION. ARCHITECT>
DUQUE MOTTA A.A // 2011. CABINS>
164 SQM // 12 GUESTS // 4 BEDROOMS
// 4 BATHROOMS. ADDRESS> PISCO
ELQUI, PAIHUANO, CHILE.
WWW.ELQUIDOMOS.CL

Cabañas Observatorio

PISCO ELQUI, CHILE

Elqui Domos is a small 10-year-old hotel located in the heart of Valle del Elqui, a narrow valley stretched between the Andes and the Chilean coastal range. The project's commission included remodeling seven existing domes, the restaurant-lobby and the addition of several new cabins to maximize the site's potential. The main challenge was to carry out an intervention that would improve the domes' living condition while highlighting the elements that make this hotel so unique.

Refashioning the existing rooms emphasized the role of the terrace as a main living area, and highlighted a specific sense of lightness – usually found in textile architecture – by allowing the cabins to only barely touch the ground, reminiscent of foreign artifacts used for sleeping, exploring the landscape, or staring at the stars.

For the new bedrooms, the idea was a room type that would provide a complementary alternative – with better living standards than the fabric domes – that would make better use of the available land, while maintaining and enhancing the conditions that make Elqui Domos such a special experience.

Main view of the cabins. View from the living area. Sleeping area with window to the sky. The cabins nestled in the nature.

View of the swimming pool. Night view. View of the cabin terrace. Section and floor plan. Exterior view of the cabins.

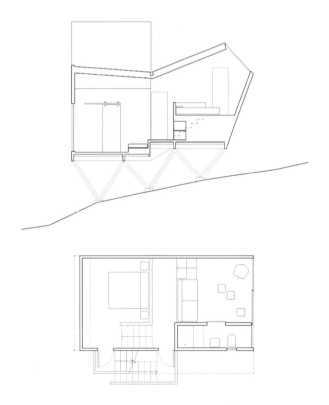

GETTING AROUND. THE AREA HAS A VARIETY OF DIFFERENT LANDSCAPES, FROM THE IMPRESSIVE NIGHT SKY TO THE AMAZING SCENE OF THE MINERAL COLORS IN THE HIGH ANDES MOUNTAINS. VISITORS CAN ENJOY NATURAL POOLS OF HOT WATER BETWEEN 32 AND 43°C OR A STROLL THROUGH THE VINEYARDS, DISTILL-ERIES, AND BEER BREWERIES, HORSE RIDING ALONGSIDE THE COCHIGUAZ RIVER, OR EXPLORING THE RICH RURAL LIFE.

INFORMATION. ARCHITECT>
JÜRGEN SEBASTIAN / WERK-
GEMEINSCHAFT LANDAU // 2014.
HOUSE, APARTMENTS> 230 SQM //
12 GUESTS // 5 BEDROOMS //
3 BATHROOMS. ADDRESS>
LEMBACHER STRASSE 13,
NOTHWEILER, GERMANY.
WWW.HAUS-AM-
GRENZGAENGERWEG.DE

Haus am Grenzgänger-weg

NOTHWEILER, GERMANY

This house has two vacation apartments: the residence house and the barn, that can be combined into a single unit, generously proportioned, light flooded, and with soft colors, directly on the border to the Alsace.

The house is an old farmhouse of 1935, complete with a residential house, stables and shed. During its renovation our motto was to combine and reconcile old and new, to maintain the old substance and to complement it with matching design elements. Natural materials, such as wooden floors, linoleum and lime plaster underscore the special flair.

Families and groups from two to twelve people find everything they need, for example well equipped kitchens, fire places and a large garden. The residential house offers room for 2–8 persons and the barn for 2–4 persons. Both are simply beautiful and practical for spending time together, also with children.

Detail of a relax corner in the renovated barn. View of the work area in the residential house. Bright kitchen. View of the kitchen and dining area in the barn.

Dining area with design furniture. View of the house from the garden. Side view.

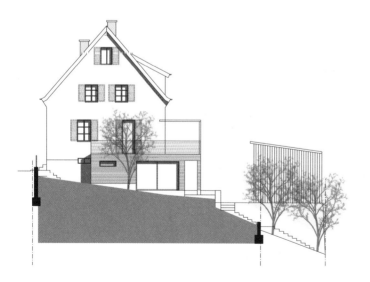

GETTING AROUND. THE HOUSE IS SITUATED IN AN ABSOLUTELY QUIET PART OF NOTHWEILER, A SMALL VILLAGE NESTLED BETWEEN THE PALATINATE FOREST AND NORTH VOSGES. EASY TO HIKE HILLS, COOL FORESTS AND EXTENSIVE ORCHARD MEADOWS PROMISE AN UNFORGETTABLE VACATION IN THE FRENCH-GERMAN BIOSPHERE RESERVE. THE AREA OFFERS ENCHANTED FORTRESSES AND ROCKS ALONG WITH VARIOUS EXCURSION SITES, SIGHTS AND SWIMMING LAKES, IDEALLY SUITED FOR HIKING, BICYCLING, MOUNTAIN CLIMBING AND TRAIL RIDING.

View of the living room in the barn. One of the bedrooms in the residential house.

INFORMATION. ARCHITECT> DL-I, DESIGNLAB-INTÉRIEURS SÀRL // 2015. 1 HOUSE AND 5 EX BARNS> 244 SQM (BARBEY), 172 SQM (ROGNEUX), 230 SQM (AGORA), 285 SQM (VOUADGÈRE) // ABOUT 8 GUESTS EACH BUILDING // 4 BEDROOMS EACH // 1 BATHROOM EACH. ADDRESS> COMMEIRE, ORSIÈRES, SWITZERLAND. WWW.MONTAGNE-ALTERNATIVE.COM

Montagne
Alternative

ORSIÈRES, SWITZERLAND

Montagne Alternative is a unique hotel concept: five former barns and a stone house located in a village in the canton of Valais were remodeled to offer a new approach to the quality of life in the authentic Swiss Alps.

The architects retained the volumes, materials and character of the original buildings, and enlarged the openings enough to allow guests to enjoy the panoramic views of the surrounding natural scenery.

The central building offers room for common activities, such as the restaurant, the lobby, the conference room, and the yoga room.

Detail of the window in the living space. Main view of one building. Detail of the new large window, that mark the original façade. View of the living room, opened on the dining area and kitchen.

*The bedroom with a great view. One of the barns,
nestled in the snowy surrounding landscape.*

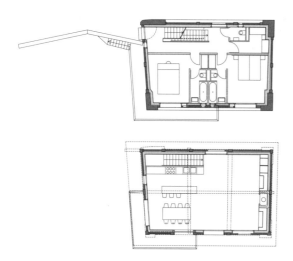

GETTING AROUND. THE AIR IS PURE, EVERYTHING IS QUIET. ALL YOU HEAR IS THE SONG OF THE CRICKETS IN THE FIELDS OF FLOWERS DURING THE SUMMER OR THE INVISIBLE WHITE OWL WHISTLING AND CHANTING IN THE SNOW IN WINTER.
THE MOUNTAIN'S PEAKS ARE REALLY CLOSE. YOU CAN HIKE, FLY WITH THE EAGLES, DESCEND WITH MOUNTAIN BIKES, CLIMB VERY HIGH, AND SLIDE THROUGH THE POWDERY SNOW.
YOU CAN UNWIND AND RELAX IN OUR PEACEFUL ROOMS, IMMERSED BY THE AUTHENTICITY OF THE SITE.

INFORMATION. ARCHITECTS> STUDIO WG3 // 2010–2014. MOBILE CABIN> 19 SQM // 2-4 GUESTS // 1 BEDROOM // 1 BATHROOM. ADDRESS> ALL OVER THE WORLD. WWW.HYPERCUBUS.AT

Hypercubus

ALL OVER THE WORLD

The Hypercubus concept is based on three fundamental principles: the use of outdoor areas with available infrastructure (alternatively also self-sufficient), the construction of small modular living units that are transportable, and the creation of a new concept in tourism (the prepaid apartment) with a uniform corporate design.

Named after the mathematical hypercube shape, the Hypercubus is a mobile hotel room. Essentially, the project reinterprets the "hotel" concept. The Hypercubus is designed in such a way that it can be totally independent technically; installation can be temporary and several Hypercubus units can be grouped into clusters.

They can be easily transported, meaning that Hypercubuses can be used on a seasonal basis and according to demand, moving around according to where they are most needed. The project offers an instant tourism infrastructure in the respective region. The "minimal housing" apartments use existing resources, are transportable thanks to their mobile construction, and are used where they are needed depending on the season.

View of the main entrance of the cabin. Side view. Section. Interior details.

GETTING AROUND. KAKSLAUTTANEN ARCTIC RESORT IS LOCATED NEXT TO URHO KEKKONEN NATIONAL PARK. IN THE WINTER GUESTS CAN EXPERIENCE THE ARCTIC WILDERNESS ON REINDEER, HUSKY, HORSE AND SNOWMOBILE SAFARIS. THE AREA IS ALSO KNOWN FOR ITS WORLD-CLASS CROSS-COUNTRY SKIING TRACKS AND SCENERY. DURING THE SUMMER AND AUTUMN VISITORS CAN ENJOY E.G. HIKING, BIKING, GOLD PANNING, HORSEBACK RIDING AND CANOEING. GUESTS CAN ALSO LEARN YEAR-AROUND ABOUT THE FASCINATING CULTURE OF THE SÁMI, THE ONLY INDIGENOUS PEOPLE IN THE EUROPEAN UNION AREA. AND OF COURSE, SANTA CLAUS & MRS. SANTA WELCOME VISITORS TO THEIR HOME EVERY SEASON.

View from above of the Glass Igloos. Main view of the Celebration House. Interior view of the Igloo Bar.

INFORMATION. ARCHITECTS>
KAKSLAUTTANEN ARCTIC RESORT //
SINCE 1974. HOTEL> 500 HECTARES //
450 GUESTS // 190 BEDROOMS //
190 BATHROOMS. ADDRESS>
KIILOPÄÄNTIE 9, SAARISELKÄ,
FINLAND.
WWW.KAKSLAUTTANEN.FI

*Night view of the Kelo-Glass Igloo. Interior view of
the Kelo-Glass Igloo.*

Kakslauttanen Arctic Resort

SAARISELKÄ, FINLAND

Kakslauttanen Arctic Resort is the world's leading arctic resort located 250 kilometers north of the Arctic Circle in Finnish Lapland. Since 1974, the resort has been offering incredible beauty of the arctic wilderness in high-quality facilities.

The resort is filled with unique marvels of arctic architecture and design. Nearly everything, from the accommodation units and restaurants to the interior decorations and furniture, is designed and made by local craftsmen and artists. Most of the buildings are designed and initiated by the owner and founder Jussi Eiramo himself, including the iconic Glass Igloos, which he invented in 1999. Made of thermal glass they keep guests warm and let them admire the arctic sky and the northern lights, even during freezing temperatures. In 2017, a 30-meter high Glass Igloo Tower will be opened, offering breathtaking views overlooking the surrounding arctic wilderness, bringing guests even closer to the arctic sky.

INFORMATION. ARCHITECT>
VINCENT VAN DUYSEN ARCHITECTS //
2010. TOWNHOUSE> 360 SQM //
6 GUESTS // 3 BEDROOMS //
2 BATHROOMS. ADDRESS>
GRAANMARKT 13, ANTWERP, BELGIUM.
WWW.GRAANMARKT13.BE/EN/
APARTMENT/THE-APARTMENT

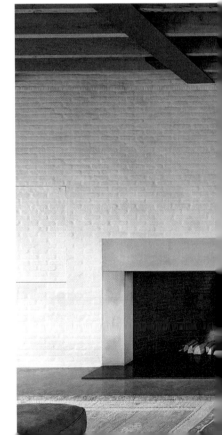

Graanmarkt 13

ANTWERP, BELGIUM

Graanmarkt 13 is designed as a welcoming and warm home, where everyone should feel at ease, offering a restaurant, a shop, a gallery space, and an apartment all under one roof. The remarkable concept occupies an entire townhouse in the center of Antwerp.

The traditional building was reworked by Vincent Van Duysen, one of Belgian's best architects. In the past years, owners Tim Van Geloven and Ilse Cornelissens turned Graanmarkt 13 into a household name, but wisely kept one of its secrets to themselves.

The initial idea was also to include a bed & breakfast on the top floors. But Tim and Ilse changed their minds and decided to turn all available space into a single luxurious apartment. Described as "their best kept secret", the apartment is now also available for rent.

Detail from the bedroom's corner. View of the bathroom with bathtub. Living area. View of the dining area with fireplace.

View of living and dining area. Detail of the bedroom. Balcony with view of the city. Floor plans. View of the kitchen and dining area.

GETTING AROUND. ANTWERP IS ALL ABOUT THE MIX: AVANT-GARDE AND ESTABLISHMENT, GLOBAL AND LOCAL, WHERE THE HEROES RANGE FROM PETER PAUL RUBENS TO DRIES VAN NOTEN. THE OLD CITY CENTER IS STEEPED IN HISTORY FROM ANCIENT FAÇADES ON NARROW STREETS TO THE IMPOSING GRAND-PLACE. THE PLANTIN-MORETUS MUSEUM IS THE ONLY MUSEUM IN THE WORLD CLASSIFIED AS A UNESCO WORLD HERITAGE SITE. IN THE SHADOW OF THE CATHEDRAL OF OUR LADY, THE CITY TEEMS WITH LIFE IN INTIMATE PUBS AND RESTAURANTS.

GETTING AROUND. LOCATED IN THE INNTAL AT THE FOOT OF THE TYROLIAN WILDER KAISER, NEAR THE WENDELSTEIN, THE ROMANTIC LOCATION RIGHT NEXT TO THE AUERBACH OFFERS ALL TYPES OF OUTDOOR FUN – SKIING, TOBOGGANING, HIKING, CLIMBING, SWIMMING NATURE, MOUNTAIN BIKING, TENNIS, SAILING, HORSEBACK RIDING, GOLF, AND MUCH MORE. DAYTRIPS ARE POSSIBLE TO THE CHIEMSEE, SALZBURG, MUNICH, OR INNSBRUCK. THE AREA ALSO OFFERS MANY CULTURAL ACTIVITIES AND EVENTS.

Exterior view from the garden. Detail of the wooden terrace. Winter side view. Living room with double height.

INFORMATION. ARCHITECTS>
ARNHARD UND ECK ARCHITEKTEN //
2014. HOUSE> 101 SQM //
2–4 GUESTS // 1 BEDROOM AND
1 GALLERY // 1 BATHROOM.
ADDRESS> ROSENWEG 10A,
OBERAUDORF, GERMANY.
WWW.GUT-FEELING.ME

*Main view of the house, with large window.
Floor plans.*

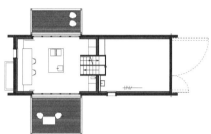

Holzhaus am Auerbach

OBERAUDORF, GERMANY

Our intention was to create an individual location as a retreat from the stress of everyday life, a place to regain one's peace of mind and to experience life's intensity at a reduced place. Already by entering the house guests should experience the intensity of the solid structure: massive wood, clay bricks and clay plaster covering the wall heating system. Finally the walls are painted with natural pigments that let the walls flex the different lights.

The house is only four-meter wide and thirteen-meter long and divided according to the split level principle. The kitchen and dining, living, and sleeping areas are open and connected via narrow stairs. The living area is a retreat for listening to music, reading, watching movies, or enjoying the view with a wood burning stove that spreads warmth, the pleasant sound of crackling and the smell of wood across the entire house. The gallery above the living room offers wellness with a free-standing bathtub with a view of the sky, complemented by a cozy reading corner. The kitchen and bathroom are also fully equipped.

GETTING AROUND. PLANNED FROM 1925 TO 1930 BY BRUNO TAUT, THE HUFEISENSIEDLUNG (HORSESHOE ESTATE) IN SOUTHERN BERLIN IS AN ICON OF NEW OBJECTIVITY. ITS MIX OF HOUSES, GARDENS AND RESIDENTIAL BLOCKS INVITES VISITORS TO GO FOR EXTENSIVE STROLLS. AT ITS CENTER IS THE HORSESHOE, A 350-METER LONG CURVED BUILDING THAT LENT THE ESTATE ITS NAME. IT WAS DECLARED A UNESCO WORLD HERITAGE SITE IN 2008. VISITORS ARE IMPRESSED NOT ONLY BY THE EXPRESSIVE COLORS BUT ALSO BY THE GREAT VARIATIONS OF THE ESTATE THAT IS CONNECTED TO THE CITY BY SUBWAY.

Kitchen with original reconstructed furniture.
Aerial view from the Hufeisensiedlung. Main view
of the house from the garden, with typical fruit trees.
View of the living and dining area.

Work area with historic tiled stove.
Upper and ground floor plans.

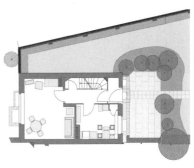

INFORMATION. ARCHITECTS>
BRUNO TAUT, KATRIN LESSER +
BEN BUSCHFELD (RESTORATION
AND INTERIORS) // 1930 AND 2012.
HOUSE> 65 SQM // 2–4 GUESTS //
2 BEDROOMS // 1 BATHROOM.
ADDRESS> BERLIN, GERMANY.
WWW.TAUTSHOME.COM

Taut's Home

BERLIN, GERMANY

The name of the house, which is part of Berlin's famous Hufeisen-siedlung, was chosen by the two owners as a reference to the name of its architect. It can be rented by architecture and design fans who want to authentically and leisurely delve into the Avantgarde construction of the 1920s.

Enthusiastically received by guests and experts, the carefully designed house in the Bauhaus style already received various monument awards. The compact, but surprisingly functional design of the cuboid house with front garden accommodates three rooms, kitchen and bathroom that were all restored in the typical cheerful colors.

All furniture and furnishings are either originally from the 1920s or were built based on historical models. The skillfully arranged interior design signifies the special pioneering atmosphere of the era's design, art and society.

INFORMATION. ARCHITECTS> ARNOLD / WERNER ARCHITEKTEN // 2011. HOUSE> 300 SQM // 5–8 GUESTS // 4 BEDROOMS // 2 BATHROOMS. ADDRESS> WALCHENSEE, GERMANY. WWW.ALPENCHALET-WALCHENSEE.DE

Walchensee Mountain Lodge

WALCHENSEE, GERMANY

Arnold / Werner have remodeled an existing lodge from the 1970s, located in the picturesque village of Walchensee in the Bavarian Alps.

The ambition was to carve out the existing quality of the architecture and create a modern and comfortable mountain lodge with great views of the lake and mountains.

The mountain lodge offers a very comfortable living environment, even during the extremely cold winter months. The six-meter high living room is connected with the kitchen area, creating a large open-plan space.

Every visible surface is covered with radial pine veneer boards. All wooden furniture was designed and produced by the architects.

GETTING AROUND. WALCHENSEE OR LAKE WALCHEN IS THE DEEPEST LAKE IN GERMANY WITH A MAXIMUM DEPTH OF 190 METERS. IT IS ALSO ONE OF THE LARGEST ALPINE LAKES MEASURING 16.4 SQUARE KILOMETERS. LOCATED SOUTH OF MUNICH IN THE BAVARIAN ALPS, IT OFFERS NATURE AND SPORTS LOVERS A VAST ARRAY OF LEISURE ACTIVITIES.

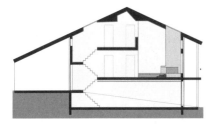

View of the surrounding nature from the kitchen.
Floor plan. Cross section.

Detail of the bathroom with exposed concrete.
View of the dining and living room.
Interior view of the bathroom.

GETTING AROUND. NOT A CROWDED SPOT FOR SURE! INSTEAD, THE TRUE COUNTRY EXPERIENCE IN THE MANY UNTOUCHED LANDSCAPES AND RICE FIELDS. COMPORTA OFFERS SURFING LESSONS, KAYAKING AND HOT BALLOON RIDES ALONG WITH HORSEBACK RIDING ON DESERTED BEACHES TO BIRD WATCHING AND CATAMARAN SAILING SURROUNDED BY DOLPHINS. THE FOOD IS ALSO AS GOOD AS IT GETS: FRESH FISH FROM THE ATLANTIC AND PORTUGUESE WINE PROVIDE FOR A TRUE GASTRONOMIC EXPERIENCE.

Interior courtyard with sand floor and wooden planks
Detail of the bathroom. The dining area. One of the
three bedrooms, with view to the garden.

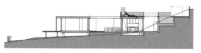

Main view of the house and garden. The top terrace with private heated pool. Cross sections.

INFORMATION. ARCHITECT>
PEDRO FERREIRA PINTO // 2011.
HOUSE> 315 SQM // 6 GUESTS //
3 BEDROOMS // 3 BATHROOMS.
ADDRESS> PEGO BEACH, COMPORTA,
PORTUGAL.
WWW.CASADOPEGO.COM

Casa do Pego

COMPORTA, PORTUGAL

Casa do Pego is a perpetual art project. This simple yet luxurious house has a unique, clean architecture, with concrete, large glass windows, and pine wood decks.

It is located in Comporta, one of the most exclusive areas of Portugal five minutes by foot from award-winning Pego Beach. The fully equipped house has three bedrooms for six people and is just one hour away from Lisbon.

The eclectic interior design features iconic mid-century modern classics along with rustic elements, creating an "out of the box" environment. The suspended fireplace and heated floors make it irresistible throughout the year, ideal for off-season breaks.

A sunny terrace with a stunning private heated pool lies on top of the house. The garden merges with the surrounding territory. It is sculptured like a sand dune, with typical beach flora and native species, such as pine tree with effortless, unpretentious landscaping.

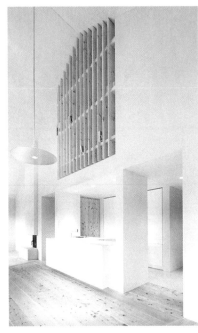

INFORMATION. ARCHITECTS> PEDEVILLA ARCHITECTS + ARCH. CAROLINE WILLEIT // 2013. HOUSE> 200 SQM // 6–8 GUESTS // 2 BEDROOMS // 1 BATHROOM. ADDRESS> PLISCIA 13, ENNEBERG MAREBBE, SOUTH TYROL, ITALY. WWW.LAPEDEVILLA.IT

View of the bright perforated wall, which works as a library. The perforated wall from the living room. View of the typical pitched roof. Main view of the house.

Chalet la Pedevilla

SOUTH TYROL, ITALY

The cultural landscape of the Val Badia in the heart of the Dolomites is distinguished by its many hamlets called "viles" that developed in various shapes on its slopes in the course of centuries. Viles are small groups of farms that formed a close-knit community. Most of the old farms consisted of two buildings, a residence and a farm building.

The vacation building ensemble was designed with reference to the building tradition of the "viles." The two buildings have regional ornaments and characteristic features and were constructed from limited local materials (Dolomite rock, solid Swiss stone pine and larch wood).

Warm timber and soft materials coupled with white exposed concrete create a protective and homey atmosphere that is in contrast to the sometimes rough climate.

Its own water spring, geothermal energy, passive solar energy and a photovoltaic system make the building independent in terms of energy consumption.

Side view of the house, nestled in the surrounding landscape. Detail of the dining area with a unique view of the mountains.

Detail of the sleeping area. View from the stairway. Detail of the stairs in warm pine wood, as most of the furniture. Floor plan.

GETTING AROUND. THE DOLOMITES ARE RENOWNED FOR SKIING IN THE WINTER MONTHS AND MOUNTAIN CLIMBING, HIKING, CYCLING, PARA-GLIDING, AND HANG GLIDING IN SUMMER AND LATE SPRING/EARLY AUTUMN. BRUNECK IS THE MAIN CITY IN THE PUSTERTAL REGION, WHILE ST. VIGIL/ENNEBERG IS THE MAIN TOURIST RESORT OF THE VAL BADIA. KRONPLATZ MOUNTAIN IS AN ATTRACTION DURING BOTH WINTER AND SUMMER. OTHER HIGHLIGHTS INCLUDE TWO LOCATIONS OF THE MESSNER MOUNTAIN MUSEUM (RIPA AND CORONES).

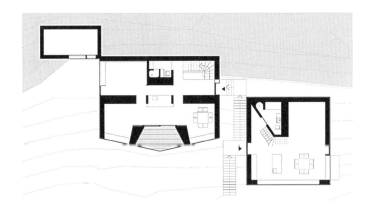

GETTING AROUND. THE HOUSE IS LOCATED IN THE SOUTHERN PART OF THY NATIONAL PARK, DENMARK. THE AREA IS KNOWN FOR ITS MAGNIFICENT NATURE AND FRESH FISH FROM THE OCEAN. THE COLD-WATER SURF CONDITION, WITH GREAT SURF SPOTS LOCATED AT THE COASTLINE FROM AGGER TO VIGSØ, IS ALSO CALLED COLD HAWAII. IN THE NATIONAL PARK ARE FRESH WATER LAKES OFFERING PERFECT BATHING CONDITION FOR SMALL KIDS. THE AREA OFFERS MANY OUTDOOR ACTIVITIES.

View of the open dining area with the long table. Detail of the fireplace and the large windows in the living room. Exterior view. View of the annex building with the bedrooms.

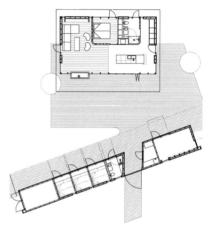

Main view of the kitchen and dining area with large windows. Floor plan.

INFORMATION. ARCHITECT>
SØREN SARUP, PURAS // 2008. HOUSE>
125 SQM // 8 GUESTS // 5 BEDROOMS
// 2 BATHROOMS. ADDRESS> AGGER,
DENMARK.
WWW.AAVEGO.DK

Aavego

AGGER, DENMARK

In Agger, by the North Sea, in the middle of fjords, lakes and dunes this vacation home offers a special Nordic bond with nature, use of light, and esthetic and functional openness.

Situated eight hundred meters from the North Sea, the house consists of three main elements – an annex building, a wooden terrace, and the main building.

The main house consists of an entrance, bathroom, an open kitchen with a dinner table, a living room with a fireplace, and a bedroom. The annex has four bedrooms with four double beds and direct access to the terrace in addition to a bathroom, a laundry room, and a private storage room.

The 180-square-meter wooden terrace is designed with many corners and small areas offering shadow, shelter, sun, protection, and comfort during all seasons. The southern façade of the main house is equipped with a large folding door that creates a direct opening from the kitchen to the large terrace.

INFORMATION. ARCHITECT> MANUEL AIRES MATEUS // 2010. 4 HUTS> 180 SQM // 8 GUESTS // 4 BEDROOMS // 4 BATHROOMS. ADDRESS> SÍTIO DA CARRASQUEIRA, COMPORTA, PORTUGAL. WWW.CASASNAAREIA.COM

Casas na Areia

COMPORTA, PORTUGAL

Casas na Areia is located one hour south of Lisbon, in Comporta, Portugal. This region is known for magnificent white sandy beaches, wine, fresh fish, rice paddies, and pine trees.

In this project by architect Manuel Aires Mateus, the sand used for the interior is the unifying element between indoors and outdoors, acting like an extension of the natural environment.

This project, conceived over the "innocence" of old local buildings, confirms the paradigm that happiness is based on the intelligent use of simplicity. To recover the soul of the existing constructions while respecting the local traditions, four separate houses were built: two of wood and reeds, and the other two in white concrete, all with thatched roofs – local material harvested on the banks of river Sado.

The huts were built by António Pinela, a local artisan, who has to renew the reeds and thatch every six to eight years.

Living area with sand floor. Main view of the cabin in white concrete. General view of three cabins. Exterior view of the swimming pool and the cabin built in wood and reeds.

Frontal view of the two cabins built in white concrete.
Detail of the white bathroom. View of the swimming
pool. Floor plan of the two typologies of cabins.
Dining area with sand floor.

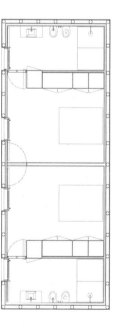

GETTING AROUND. CASAS NA AREIA
IS LOCATED NEAR THE SMALL FISHING
VILLAGE OF CARRASQUEIRA. IT IS
CLOSE TO THE UNIQUE PALAFITTE
PORT OF CARRASQUIERA – A JETTY
ON STILTS. THE REGION IS PART OF
THE NATURAL RESERVE OF RIVER
SADO, OFFERING MAGNIFICENT
SUNSETS AND BREATHTAKING VIEWS
OF THE RIVER. IT IS HOME TO A
GREAT VARIETY OF WILDLIFE SUCH AS
FLAMINGOS, STORKS AND DOLPHINS
AND ONE OF THE BEST PLACES IN
PORTUGAL FOR BIRD WATCHING.

Rio Marie

BERLIN, GERMANY

The Brazilian Oscar Niemeyer constructed a social housing block in 1957 in the Hansaviertel of Berlin on the occasion of the Interbau fair. Having been converted to condominiums in the meantime, a 4-room apartment was due for renovation in 2012.

After opening up the floor plan it was turned into a surprisingly open modern apartment with a generous living/dining area, two well-proportioned bedrooms with dressing areas and two bathrooms. The sliding doors feature the façade pattern of the elevator as homage to the 1950s, while Brazilian rosewood pays tribute to the home country of the architect.

The thin materials and extended legs of the furniture are reminiscent of the era when luxuries were rare. Linoleum, stoneware tiles, slim door handles by Johannes Potente are combined with contemporary items – the renovation has firmly established the apartment in the 21st century.

View of the workplace with bookcase under the large windows. View of the kitchen. Dining area with Brazilian jacaranda wall.

INFORMATION. ARCHITECTS>
A-BASE | BÜRO FÜR ARCHITEKTUR //
2012. APARTMENT> 4 GUESTS //
2 BEDROOMS // 2 BATHROOMS.
ADDRESS> ALTONAERSTRASSE 10,
BERLIN, GERMANY.
WWW.ROOMBERGS.DE

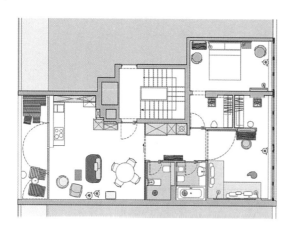

GETTING AROUND. THE OSCAR-NIEMEYER-HAUS IS IN THE IMMEDIATE VICINITY OF SCHLOSS BELLEVUE, THE OFFICIAL RESIDENCE OF THE GERMAN FEDERAL PRESIDENT AS WELL AS SEVERAL OTHER PROMINENT POLITICAL AND CULTURAL HIGHLIGHTS OF BERLIN. ONLY ONE URBAN TRAIN STATION AWAY FROM THE NEW CENTRAL STATION, TWO STATIONS FROM THE ZOO AND YET IN THE MIDDLE OF GREENERY SURROUNDED BY THE TIERGARTEN PARK, THE GREEN LUNG IN THE HEART OF THE CITY, IT IS THE IDEAL STARTING POINT FOR MANY LEISURE ACTIVITIES.

View of the sleeping area and living room with loggia. Floor plan. Exterior view of the Oscar-Niemeyer-Haus, built during the Internationale Bauausstellung (IBA) in Berlin 1957.

The kitchen with 1950s details and modern floating kitchen block. View of the workplace. Living room in blue tones.

GETTING AROUND. THE CAMPER CABINS ARE LOCATED WITHIN THE 456-ACRE WHITETAIL WOODS REGIONAL PARK, PART OF EMPIRE TOWNSHIP IN DAKOTA COUNTY AND ONE-MILE NORTH OF THE VERMILLION RIVER. THE PARK FEATURES LOW-IMPACT SKI AND WALKING TRAILS, A DESIGNED "DRY CREEK" TO HANDLE SURFACE WATER RUNOFF, THE FAWN CROSSING NATURE PLAY AREA AND THE EMPIRE LAKE SHELTER PICNIC AREA.

Exterior view of the cabins nestled into the Whitetail Woods Regional Park. Side view. Chill area with big windows.

INFORMATION. ARCHITECTS> HAMMEL, GREEN AND ABRAHAMSON // 2015. 3 CAMPER CABINS> 21 SQM EACH // 4–6 GUESTS PER CABIN // 1 BEDROOM // 1 SHARED BATHROOM. ADDRESS> 17100 STATION TRAIL, FARMINGTON, EMPIRE TOWNSHIP IN DAKOTA COUNTY, MINNESOTA, USA. WWW.CO.DAKOTA.MN.US/PARKS/ PARKSTRAILS/WHITETAILWOODS/ PAGES/WHITETAIL-WOODS-CAMPER-CABINS.ASPX

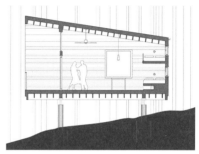

Exterior view of the cabins. Cross section.

Whitetail Woods Regional Park Camper Cabins

MINNESOTA, USA

Nestled into the hillside of Whitetail Woods Regional Park within the Minneapolis/St. Paul metropolitan area, Hammel, Green and Abrahamson, Inc. designed three new camper cabins. The cabins weave their way into a stand of pine trees and serve as a key amenity in the first phase of the parks master plan.

While the basic concept is based on a treehouse, the cabins are accessible to all by building "houses in the trees" that can be entered from a bridge at the crest of the hill next to ski and hiking trails. The cabins provide ample space, electricity, lighting, heat and natural ventilation with framed views into the surrounding forest, bringing modern comfort to the outdoor adventurer.

Two full-size bunks with built-in storage, dining and sitting areas provide accommodations for four individuals while a sleeper sofa and additional folding seating can comfortably accommodate six. The cabins are supported by a nearby bathhouse.

INFORMATION. ARCHITECT>
JENNIFER BENINGFIELD OF
OPENSTUDIO ARCHITECTS // 2014.
HOUSE> 8 GUESTS // 4 BEDROOMS
// 3 BATHROOMS. ADDRESS>
DE VILLIERS STREET, PRINCE ALBERT,
SOUTH AFRICA.
WWW.PERFECTHIDEAWAYS.CO.ZA/
DETAILS/SWARTBERG-HOUSE

The house at night under the Milky Way. Main bathroom with slots and shutters. View of the double-height space of the living room.

Swartberg House

PRINCE ALBERT, SOUTH AFRICA

"The eternal stillness of the Karoo is balm to the soul. It is a place where the stresses of urban life evaporate in the dry air, and the pace of life slows to a thoughtful stroll", Gavin Bell, Telegraph.

Designed by Openstudio Architects, and completed in 2014, this passive solar house on the edge of the Karoo desert in South Africa enjoys spectacular views of the Swartberg Mountains and incredible stars at night.

Large glazed timber doors slide into roughcast plaster brick walls, while small scattered openings are arranged to follow the positions of the stars in constellations visible from the upper roof terraces.

Ash shutters, doors and joinery contrast with the dark brick floors, which also act as solar collectors. A low-chlorine private pool surrounded by a stone enclosure is located next to a generous outdoor terrace.

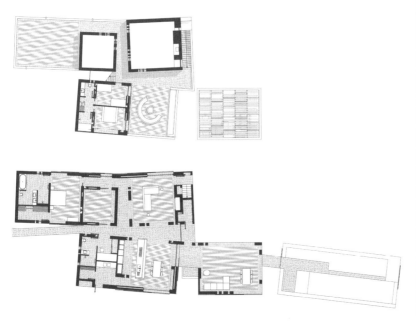

GETTING AROUND. THE HOUSE IS A TEN TO FIFTEEN MINUTE WALK FROM THE CENTER OF THE 250 YEAR-OLD TOWN OF PRINCE ALBERT, WHICH IS THE GATEWAY TO THE SWARTBERG MOUNTAINS, A UNESCO WORLD HERITAGE SITE. IT HAS A COLLECTION OF HISTORIC BUILDINGS, INCLUDING TYPICAL WHITE-WASHED KAROO DWELLINGS. THE QUALITY OF THE LIGHT ATTRACTS ARTISTS, PHOTOGRAPHERS AND STAR-GAZERS. WINE, OLIVE OIL, FIGS, PEACHES AND OTHER FRUIT ARE GROWN IN THE AREA. KAROO FOSSIL SITES AND KHOISAN PAINTINGS CAN BE VISITED WITH A LOCAL GUIDE.

View from the dining area to the Swartberg Mountains. Ground and first floor plans. Light patterns on the roughcast plaster walls.

The limewashed uneven profile of the house and the surrounding landscape. View of the upper roof terrace. The long pool enclosed by a black stone wall.

INFORMATION. ARCHITECTS> ZALIG AAN ZEE // 2013. HOUSE> 10 GUESTS // 3 BEDROOMS // 3 BATHROOMS. ADDRESS> DE JUDESTRAAT, KNOKKE-HEIST, BELGIUM. WWW.ZALIGAANZEE.BE

View of the living space, view of one of the bedrooms, the terrace from above.

Zalig Aan Zee

KNOKKE-HEIST, BELGIUM

Located in the Belgian seaside resort Knokke-Heist, this charming holiday house has been completely renovated and designed by Stefaan Van Dyck and his wife Kathleen Cassiers.

Reclaimed timber with a patina of cement, concrete floors and a color palette of black, white and sandy tones evoke an instant beach vibe and relaxed mood. The layout of the house makes it very bright because of the open-plan living room and kitchen that leads to the sunny garden and outdoor lounge.

Bedrooms and bathrooms are located across the first floor. The sleeping loft under the gable with its built-in beds and an additional pull-out bed in reclaimed wood is a paradise for children. The house can easily accommodate up to ten people. Ideal for a weekend with family and friends. Zalig Aan Zee offers six lovely holiday homes on the Belgian Coast for ten to twenty people, all in the typical "Zalig Aan Zee" style.

GETTING AROUND. KNOKKE-HEIST IS A VERY FASHIONABLE SEASIDE RESORT ON THE BELGIAN COAST LESS THAN 20 KILOMETERS FROM BRUGGE. IT OFFERS SUN, SEA AND BEACH, BUT ALSO MAGNIFICENT WOODS, POLDERS AND DUNES, IDEALLY SUITED FOR WATER SPORTS, GOLF, AND CYCLING BUT ALSO CATCHING CRABS AT THE PIER OR BUILDING SANDCASTLES. FROM BISTRO PUB TO BRASSERIE TO GOURMET RESTAURANT, ART GALLERIES, FASHION BOUTIQUES, DESIGN SHOPS AND FRESH BAKERIES CAN ALL BE FOUND IN THIS VIBRANT SEASIDE RESORT.

View of the kitchen and dining area. Detail of the sleeping area.

GETTING AROUND. THERE ARE GREAT PLACES IN BASEL TO RELAX AND HAVE GOOD FOOD AND DRINKS. THE CONSUM BAR IS OFFERING SALAMI AND CHEESE SPECIALTIES AND MORE THAN 100 DIFFERENT WINES AT THE CENTER OF THE HISTORIC DISTRICT OF KLEINBASEL. IN THE VOLTA BRÄU THE URBAN CHARACTER OF A BAR MEETS THE ARTISAN CONGENIALITY OF A BREWERY WITH AN INTEGRATED BREW HOUSE. DURING THE SUMMER MONTHS, SNACK TALLS – BUVETTEN – INVITE PASSERSBY TO LINGER ON THE BANK OF THE RHINE RIVER.

View of the common living room. View of the dining area. Interior view of the boutique hotel. One of the bedrooms with colorful carpet.

View to the relax area with wooden floor, walls and ceiling. Floor plans.

INFORMATION. ARCHITECTS> BUCHNER BRÜNDLER ARCHITEKTEN AND GREGO // 2016. BOUTIQUE HOTEL> 1,500 SQM // 65 BEDROOMS // 65 BATHROOMS. ADDRESS> BRUNNGÄSSLEIN 8, BASEL, SWITZERLAND. WWW.NOMAD.CH

Nomad

BASEL, SWITZERLAND

The unique architecture by the Buchner Bründler architecture team provided powerful specifications for the structure and atmosphere of the Hotel Nomad with the careful renovation of the apartment house of the 1950s with its many small divisions and the radical exposed concrete appendix in the courtyard.

The interior design concept by GREGO countered the rigid expression of the architecture with equally powerful softness and comfort. With the prototypical woven fabric of the Kilim carpet in contemporary colors and patterns and with a customized furniture collection also made of Kilim, the interior design creates a unique atmosphere with a strong sensual identity and directness that corre-sponds to the sculptural radicalism of the solid in-situ concrete.

The interior design of the completely different room typologies in the two parts of the house is a reaction to the architecture and combines with it into a distinctive one-of-a-kind locality.

INFORMATION. ARCHITECTS>
JARMUND / VIGSNÆS AS
ARKITEKTER MNAL // 2015. TOURIST
CABIN> 200 SQM MAIN CABIN,
70 SQM SECONDARY RESCUE HUT //
AROUND 30 GUESTS // 7 BEDROOMS
// 1 BATHROOM. ADDRESS>
OKSTINDAN, HAMNES, NORDLAND,
NORWAY.
WWW.UT.NO/HYTTE/3.1933/

Rabot Tourist Cabin

NORDLAND, NORWAY

The cabin is named after the French glaciologist and geographer Charles Rabot who explored the local mountains in the 1880s. It was planned and built with local materials and local commitment.

The main cabin is an eye-catching yet neutral volume with a diagonal spatial concept. The snow and heavy winds at the site, determined the simple shape of the cabin, without protruding elements. The two entrances on two opposite sides feature restrooms, firewood and food storage areas.

In the center of the cabin, a spacious mezzanine level creates an intimate space for the kitchen underneath. Placed diagonally to the kitchen, there are two spacious common areas with double-height ceiling and large window surfaces. The characteristic windows open in two directions, towards the mountain range and towards the mountain plateau and the valley. By contrast, the various bedrooms have smaller windows framing the surroundings.

One of the common areas from above.
Main view of the cabin. Detail of the large window from outside. View of the common area with large window surfaces.

View of the kitchen and dining room. Sleeping area.
Night view. Floor plans. Main view of the cabin
covered by timber boards with a coarse finish, treated
with ferric sulphate for a gray natural feel.

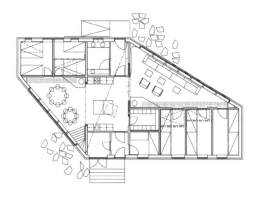

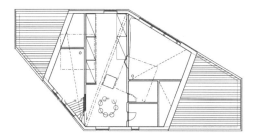

GETTING AROUND. THE RABOT
TOURIST CABIN IS ONE OF MANY DNT
(NORWEGIAN TREKKING ASSOCIA-
TION) LODGING FACILITIES THROUGH-
OUT NORWAY. IT IS LOCATED AT 1200
METERS ABOVE SEA LEVEL, CLOSE
TO THE GLACIER AT OKSTINDAN IN
NORTHERN NORWAY. THE SITE IS
SPECTACULAR WITH THE MOUNTAINS
AND GLACIERS IN CLOSE PROXIMITY.
THE WEATHER CAN BE EXTREMELY
HARSH AND THE STRUCTURE IS CON-
STRUCTED FOR HEAVY WINDS AND
STORM. THE SITE IS ONLY ACCESSIBLE
BY FOOT OR ON SKIS.

GETTING AROUND. KANCHANABURI IS THE LARGEST OF THE WESTERN PROVINCES OF THAILAND. THE TOWN GAINED FAME AFTER WWII WHEN THE JAPANESE SOLDIERS USED IT AS A BASE CAMP FOR THE POWS TO BUILD THE NOTORIOUS THAI-BURMA-RAIL-WAY AND THE WELL-KNOWN BRIDGE OVER THE RIVER KWAI. THE PROVINCE IS ALSO KNOWN FOR ITS NATURE SUCH AS FOREST, MOUNTAINS, CAVES AND WATERFALLS. THE LARGE AREA OF WATER ACCOMMODATES A GREAT NUMBER OF FLOATING HOUSES AND RAFTS.

Exterior view of the floating house. Detail of the bathroom. View of the river from the terrace. The sleeping area with large window.

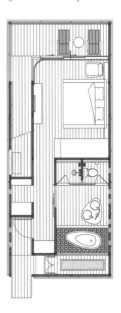

Main view of the cabins. Floor plan.

INFORMATION. ARCHITECTS>
AGALIGO STUDIO // 2015. FLOATING
HOUSE> 110 SQM // 2 GUESTS EACH
HOUSE // 1 BEDROOM EACH //
1 BATHROOM EACH. ADDRESS>
KANCHANABURI, THAILAND.
WWW.X2RESORTS.COM/RESORTS/
RIVER-KWAI

X-Float

KANCHANABURI, THAILAND

X-Float adds a new dimension of design and comfort to the River Kwai's floating houses. The unique accommodation complements the Project X2 River Kwai Resort. The design of X-Float is a cross of vernacular and modern architecture.

Situated at the river bend, all units are oriented with a maximized view of the river and the greatest possible protection from the harsh, tropical afternoon sunlight. The main structure of X-Float is made out of lightweight steel framing, clad with fiber cement siding and plywood. Wastewater and sewage are treated before being released into the river.

To facilitate water filtration and reinforce the surrounding ecosystem, aquatic plants such as reed, papyrus, and pondweed were planted around the site.

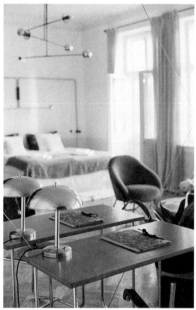

INFORMATION. ARCHITECT>
MATEUSZ BAUMILLER // 2015.
APARTMENT> 180 SQM //
8–12 GUESTS // 4 BEDROOMS //
4 BATHROOMS. ADDRESS>
LWOWSKA 17/7, WARSAW, POLAND.
WWW.AUTORROOMS.PL

*Living room with furniture from young polish
designers. Details of the sleeping area. The historical
apartment building situated in the hip district of
Warsaw. Bedroom in white with brass details and
glass shower.*

Autor Rooms

WARSAW, POLAND

In July 2015, Autor Warsaw Rooms, located in a beautiful, historic apartment building in the very center of Warsaw, Poland, announced its grand opening.

Offering a unique take on nightly accommodations, the concept's initiator and host, Warsaw's well-known graphic design studio Mamastudio, invited Starter Gallery and a long list of independent young creative professionals from the world of Polish design, fashion, crafts and culinary arts to take part in the project.

The objective was to create a space where guests feel as comfortable as visiting close friends. Friends who not only provide a high standard of accommodation, but who are also excellent hosts in an evolving city full of life, creativity and interesting people.

Bedroom with chill area and large balcony. View of another bedroom with a wooden box-bathroom.

View of the kitchen. Bathroom with a large mirror.
Details of the bedroom.

GETTING AROUND. AUTOR ROOMS IS LOCATED IN THE HIP ŚRÓDMIEŚCIE DISTRICT. IT IS SURROUNDED BY CAFES, BARS, RESTAURANTS AND GALLERIES. MOST ATTRACTIONS SUCH AS PALACE OF CULTURE, ŁAZIENKI PARK, NATIONAL GALLERY AND THE OLD TOWN CAN BE REACHED BY FOOT OR BY PUBLIC TRANSPORTATION IN A FEW MINUTES. EXCURSIONS ARE ARRANGED BASED ON WHAT GUESTS WANT TO EXPERIENCE: ARCHITECTURE, DESIGN, ART, FASHION, AND FOOD. GUESTS CAN ALSO BUY OBJECTS FROM THE HOTEL'S FURNISHINGS.

INFORMATION. ARCHITECT>
JAN HENRIK JANSEN // 2016. HOUSE>
110 SQM // 6 GUESTS // 3 BEDROOMS //
2 BATHROOMS. ADDRESS> RÅBYLILLE
STRAND, MØN, DENMARK.
WWW.HAUSAUFMOEN.DE/BIRKEDAL

*Interior view of the house. One of the bedrooms with
cantilevered desk from the bed. View of the entrance
pavilion and one of the circular terraces. Exterior view
of the house from the garden.*

Birkedal

MØN, DENMARK

Located on the island of Møn, the idea was to create a house in which all rooms are round with each resulting cylinder appearing almost like a house on its own. All façades are covered in thin spruce logs. Their barks change with time to adopt various shades of gray, keeping the appearance of the logs lively for many years.

In contrast to this gray, the windows were framed with rusty Corten steel reveals. On the inside, all structuring surfaces feature different shades of white. The hues were chosen based on the wish for clearly discernible, "rural-rustic" materials and surfaces.

The walls were covered in rough-sawn strips and planks whose white paint at the same time does not hide their timber nature. All floors are covered in a mosaic of white beach pebbles. In contrast to the rather cool white, all furniture, fitting, lights, and faucets are made of warm oak and brass.

As a contrast to the soft white surfaces, fixtures and furniture are made from leather, brass and oiled oak. The three large bedrooms sleep up to six adults in bespoke oak framed beds which extend from large bay windows into the center of the rooms where headboards double as writing desks.

Exterior view of the wooden structure of the round spaces. View of the kitchen. The bright bathroom with garden view. View of the surrounding landscape from one of the three bedrooms.

GETTING AROUND. THE ISLAND OF MØN – "RÜGEN'S SMALLER SISTER" – IS CONSIDERED ONE OF DENMARK'S MOST BEAUTIFUL LOCATIONS. IN ADDITION OF CULTURAL MONU-MENTS SUCH AS BRONZE AGE BURIAL MOUNDS, MEDIEVAL CHURCHES WITH FAMOUS LIME PAINTINGS, MANORS, THE HISTORIC "ISLAND CAPITAL" STEGE AND LISELUND CAS-TLE WITH ITS ROMANTIC PARK, THE 216-SQUARE-KILOMETER ISLAND IN-CLUDES ONE OF DENMARK'S MAJOR NATURAL ATTRACTION – MØNS KLINT, WHITE CHALK CLIFFS THAT DROP STEEPLY INTO THE SEA. THE HOUSE IS ONE AND A HALF HOUR DRIVE FROM THE LAID-BACK SCANDINAVIAN DE-SIGN METROPOLIS OF COPENHAGEN.

INFORMATION. ARCHITECTS> LEAPFACTORY SRL // 2011. HUT> 29 SQM // 12 GUESTS // 1 BEDROOM. ADDRESS> FREBOUDZE GLACIER, MONTE BIANCO, COURMAYEUR, AOSTA, ITALY. WWW.BIVACCOGERVASUTTI.COM

View from above of the refuge. Living area with rounded panoramic window.

Nuova Capanna Gervasutti

COURMAYEUR, AOSTA, ITALY

The first alpine refuge of the latest generation provides the optimal combination of comfort, safety and respect for the mountain. The refuge is the pinnacle of achievement of LEAPfactory, an Italian company that designs, creates and produces modular structures with a minimal impact on the environment.

The modular construction, entirely prefabricated from high standard materials uses sophisticated technologies to handle extreme temperatures and the difficulties due to the altitude and position of the construction site.

The living area, with an extraordinary rounded panoramic window facing the valley, is equipped with a kitchen, a dining table and seating. The sleeping area has twelve bunk beds and spaces to store gear. The round shape of the building was specifically conceived to bear snow and wind loads. On the outside, the particular red and white pattern has been chosen to create an important reference point for mountaineers.

GETTING AROUND. THE NUOVA CAPANNA GERVASUTTI, IS INSTALLED ON THE FREBOUDZE GLACIER, IN FRONT OF THE SPECTACULAR EAST FACE OF THE GRANDES JORASSES OF THE MONT BLANC RANGE. THE CANTILEVERED HUT OFFERS TO ITS GUESTS STUNNING SUNRISES OVER THE GLACIER. IT CAN BE USED AS A FOOTHOLD BEFORE A MOUNTAIN ASCENT, OR AS A DESTINATION FOR EXPERT EXCURSIONISTS. THE EXPERIENCE OF SLEEPING AT 2,835 METERS, SURROUNDED BY NOTHING BUT PEAKS AND STARS, IS TRULY UNIQUE.

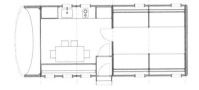

Lateral view of the cabin with the red and white pattern. View from below. Floor plan. The cabin surrounded by snow.

Map

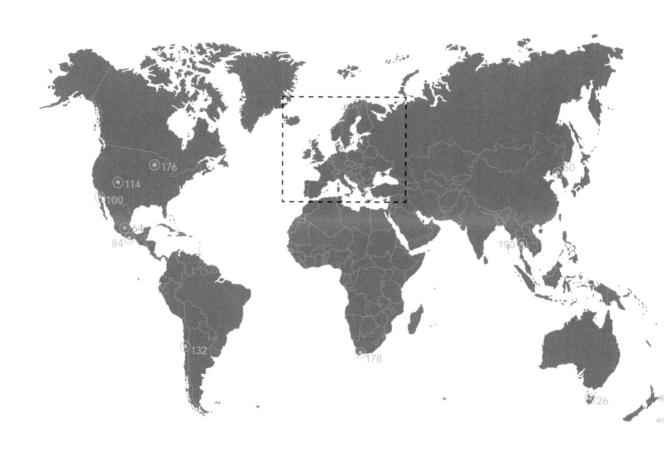

⊙ CITIES AND METROPOLISES

⊙ MOUNTAINS AND COUNTRYSIDE

⊙ SEA AND LAKES

EUROPE MAP

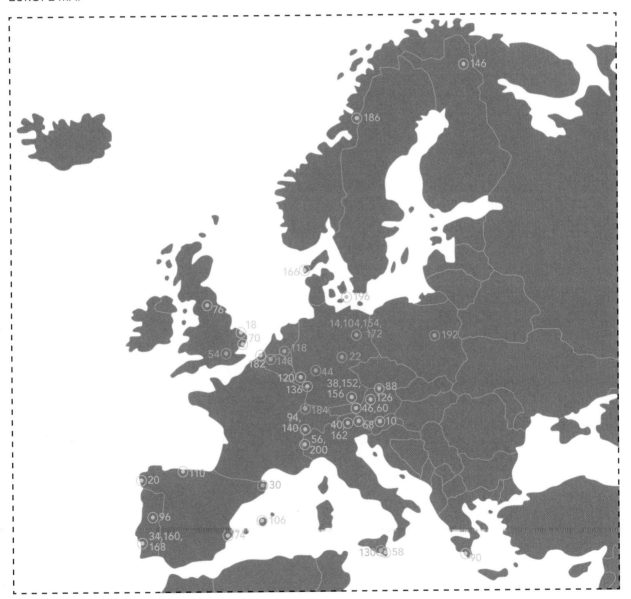

Places to go and things to do

an index of accommodations and activities

 CLIMBING

CYCLING

RESTAURANTS

GOLF

HIKING

KAYAKING

SIGHTSEEING

SAILING

SHOPPING

RIDING

SKIING

SWIMMING

WINE TASTING

 CITIES AND METROPOLISES

MAINA / GREECE
WWW.MAINA.GR

    90

MANSHAUSEN ISLAND RESORT / NORWAY
WWW.MANSHAUSEN.NO

     80

MILL HOUSE / ENGLAND
WWW.HUNSETTMILL.CO.UK

    18

PUMPHOUSE POINT / AUSTRALIA
WWW.PUMPHOUSEPOINT.COM.AU

   26

SEE 31 / AUSTRIA
WWW.TRAUNSEE31.AT

    126

TDA HOUSE / MEXICO
WWW.AIRBNB.DE/ROOMS/498808

     84

THE TRUFFLE / SPAIN
WWW.ENSAMBLE.INFO

    20

X-FLOAT / THAILAND
WWW.X2RESORTS.COM/RESORTS/ RIVER-KWAI

     190

ZALIG AAN ZEE / BELGIUM
WWW.ZALIGAANZEE.BE

     182

Picture
Credits

All other pictures were made available by the architects, designers, or hosts.